HOW TO BECOME A SUCCESSFUL AUTHOR OF BOOKS

Practical Guide on How to Become an Author
The Beginner's Guide to Taking the First Steps Into The World of Writing

By

Robert Flemingson

Table of Contents

Introduction

I see that. You're as yet apprehensive. You're ready to hit the bestseller at this moment. You read or knew about authors who had at no other time published anything and who hit with a million-merchant in their first endeavor.

The joystick is supplanted. Such discoveries are incredible news since they are so uncommon. Try not to anticipate that the lottery should be won. On the off chance that you need to go anyplace with your book and blog, ensure that you have: took in the craftsmanship, by experimentation, there is no compelling reason to compose a convincing story. Some did this for you—and read about it books. In this manner, following demonstrated techniques is the best wagered you can have.

Realize that the incredible essayists were great per users most importantly. The race has turned out to be so savage; you'll help yourself out when you comprehend what fruitful authors read before you endeavor to get a second look from a distributer. Set aside the effort to realize what you're doing. You will express gratitude toward yourself later.

Written Things Shorter Than a Book

There shouldn't be a book that you start any more than when you're a kindergarten teacher you should enroll in grade school. There's a book you're going for. Start small, learn the skills, and improve your skills.

Do some comments. Write the email. Start a blog. Have stories in a few magazines, a journal, and an e-zine. Take a class in reporting and creative writing at night or offline. Publishers are competing for network writers (in short: viewers, groups, friends, fans). And begin to build yours now. Any of the above items will begin to build momentum behind your writing and will raise the prestige of your reputation as an author.

Get out of your mind a quarter-million clichés, know what writing entails, become a specialist in something, create your site, and then start thinking about that book or novel.

Plugged Yourself into a Community of Writers

Would you think you can do this on your own?

Almost every traditionally published writer I meet is surrounded by a friendly family. How else are they going to handle things like?

- Frustration
- Discouragement
- Procrastination
- Learning that I can be helped by friends anytime I need it requires leaving the Group. Another pair of eyes on your job can prove invaluable if you start. Far better is ten pairs of eyes. Join a group of artists. Look for a tutor. Hold open to critique.

A caveat with groups of writers: ensure that at least one person, preferably the leader, is widely published and understands the landscape of publishing. Therefore, the blind leading the blind is at risk.

In this eBook we will deal with all these titles elaborately

1. **Never Try to Become an Author without going through this...**

- It's...Considered the craft and strengthened the skills

- Write less material than a novel
- Link with a network of writers

2. Writing your book

- Build a Writing Calendar
- Prepare and Program
- Keep your day job.
- Become a ruthless self-editor

3. Trying to get a good contract for writing

- How to get an agent
- Getting a distributer
- Writing the book with an editor going crazy (again).

4. You don't have to write it on your own?

- Self-publishing review
- Setting apart your book
- Selecting the correct publisher independently
- Self-publishing executioner

Chapter 1
How To Find A Topic

Most independent authors ' ultimate goal is to see their name listed as the author of a bestselling book. Sadly, it is not always a straightforward task to find subjects to write a book about. There's no way to guarantee you've selected a good subject for your book, so before you begin your novel you'll have to weigh a number of different considerations.

It's hard to write a novel without the proper help. You could end up making crucial mistakes without someone who has done it before. Anyone who says it's easy to learn how to write a novel has never done it. Unless they did, they would have known that writing a book would require much more than a useful piece of grammar code.

Writing a Memoir

At one point, actors who had lived exceptionally interesting lives were the only ones who wrote memoirs. There are memoirs today, though, covering topics ranging from raising a child with special needs and battling addiction. Several authors also sell memoirs to make a career. For example, the published memoirs of Susan Shapiro include Only as Good as Your Letter, Lighting Up, Fix-Up Fanatic Secrets, and Five People Who Broke My Heart.

If you have to share a unique story, you don't have to be known for writing a memoir. You need to be willing to share your thoughts honestly and openly, however, even if they're uncomfortable. However, a memoirist must also note that friends and family may not be in favor of seeing themselves represented unflatteringly.

Begin With an Inspiration Exercise

Writing a memoir or describing a particular period or aspect of your life is something deeply satisfying. With a few measures and exercises, build and refine the rewarding experience of writing a memoir.

The structure and concentration of a novel is close to that of a great movie. Many movies center in the life of a character on just one event or theme. For this project, making a list of five movies you enjoy is a fun way to get motivated. Answer these questions for each movie:

1. What is the protagonist's primary objective (the main character)?
2. What is the protagonist's way of getting big conflict (or conflicts)?
3. How does the main obstacle react to the protagonist? (Initially bad? Better later?)
4. How are the disputes resolved?
5. Is the hero reaching their goal?
6. How different is the protagonist at the end of the film?

Working through this process will help you arrange the memoirs in a good mindset.

Decide on the Event or Theme

It's time to get more specific about the event or theme. Which event or theme will be covered in your life? Example.

- Love and romance: you can tell the story of your romantic relationships, for example. This is an example of how a memoir can dive into each period of your life while staying focused on a single theme.
- Coming of age: this is an example of reflecting on a certain period of time. In a coming-of-age novel, your autobiography in your early

adolescence will focus exclusively on an incident or a series of events.

- Career-related drama: If you have an interesting experience working in a company or organization, you can concentrate on your background story.

Prepare Lists Using a Helpful App

Prepare cards to list event and theme-related memories. Take any notecards on notecard-styled organizer devices like Trello, whether physical or virtual. Each good story unfolds in three acts, whether memoirs or movies. Start with three notecards with the following headers (just the words in bold):

Act One-The Exposition: present yourself to the reader, the primary goal during this time of your life, and the early events leading to the major conflict at the core of your memoirs. The occurrence also pushes you to establish the primary objective.

Act two-Conflict: This is the event that changes life and is the primary source of tension. Either it's a major obstacle to a target you've already built, or it's the impetus for a new goal.

Act three — Resolution: the reader discovers in the final act how you responded to the confrontation, how you or someone else) handled it, and the closing actions that demonstrate that you improved and influenced your life by resolving the conflict.

Once you have produced a card for each act, collect as many thoughts as you can of each act during your lifetime.

Add Six More Cards

Build six more cards once you have nice long memory lists connected to each case. Write one of the six questions that you answered about the films on each card. Make a list of memories and information that react to every request. Write as many thoughts and related events as you can until you get a better idea of how these six questions would be answered in your autobiography.

Begin Writing (But Not Necessarily in Order)

Start Writing (but not always in order) Use the nine cards that you generated as layout guides. This does not necessarily mean that you must start at the beginning of the three Acts and chronologically write the book. The goal is to stop the obstruction of the author at all times. If possible, start with the most jumping activity or memory at you, shouting the loudest, "Write about me!."

Final Revisions and Word Count

Upon finishing the book, go multiple times through the whole text. Check for mistakes in spelling and grammar. Find and rewrite awkward sentences. It's a good time to get the word count down to an acceptable amount (or beefed up). The length of your autobiography could be around 80,000 words (i.e. 20 chapters each with 4,000 words). When you intend to apply to a publisher or literary agent, look for something similar to that. If the autobiography is for personal satisfaction or just for friends and family, make it as long or as brief as you like.

Tough Love Makes Good Books

If you're writing with corporate publication aspirations in mind, when you rewrite the book and apply it with a submission schedule, you'll have to be tough on yourself. Still, let the tough love arrive in the later stages of the update. The goal is to overcome the author's trap in the early stages at all times, even if the writing is poor. Do whatever is necessary to keep the writing running until the book is completed.

Did you feel depressed when you writing memoirs

While reading memoirs, feelings of sadness are more normal than you might think. Nonetheless, it is important to understand the difference between common write-related issues and the signs of a more serious mental health issue.

Causes of Depression Feelings While Memoir Writing

There are many reasons why writers can start writing their memoirs to feel depressed. Identifying the root of your problem is the first step to finding an appropriate solution.

Writer's Block

Writer block is a common cause of depression in artistic types. It's natural to experience mood changes if you feel like the one whose strategy doesn't go as well as you had planned.

While there is no definitive solution for the writer's block, it may be helpful to give yourself another idea to work on for a few days. Try to write poetry, prepare a few request emails for magazine audiences, or just post about your thoughts. A trusted writer can also help you start your creative process by curling up with a good book.

Painful memories

If your book addresses sensitive issues, coping with these painful memories on a daily basis is likely to cause certain feelings of depression. A support group is likely to provide some comfort to writers who are preparing memoirs about eating disorders, sexual abuse, domestic violence, or other traumatic events. Just as a writing group can provide valuable feedback on your job, a support group can help you feel less alone with people dealing with the same problems in your struggles. If you can't find a live support group in your neighborhood, spending some time in an online chat room related to the topic can give you enough room to wind up and get on with your task.

Past Mistakes

Most people had experiences they wish they had handled differently in their past. Perhaps they hurt the feelings of a good friend by doing something unkind during an argument, or maybe they feel like slacking their future job prospects in school are minimal. When you believe the symptoms of anxiety are linked to perceived inadequacies when reading memoirs, note that 10 to 15 years after the event happened, it is always much easier to find the right way to handle a difficult situation. Everybody makes mistakes, but sharing his/her life history frankly needs a courageous author.

When to Seek Help

Though having any depressive feelings though writing memoirs is perfectly normal, drastic and persistent shifts in your mood may suggest a more serious mental health issue. Suggest making an appointment to meet with your healthcare provider should you note the following warning signs:

- The things you normally enjoy no longer bring you satisfaction.
- You suddenly lose weight and gain weight.
- You have trouble sleeping or you are so exhausted that you always want to nap.

- The dramatic improvement in your conduct has been reflected on by your friends and family.
- You feel hopeless and useless, or you have been considering suicide.

There is no need to be ashamed if your health care provider decides that you are suffering from clinical depression. Depression is one of the most prevalent mental health disorders, and evidence suggests authors are more likely than the general population to suffer from depressive episodes. For example, Hans Christian Andersen, Tennessee Williams, Robert Louis Stevenson, and F. Scott Fitzgerald is just a few of the many authors who have been dealing over the years with depression. Through Unholy Ghost: Depression books, 22 authors representing different genres further address the topic by exploring how their careers have been affected by depression.

While it is by no means an easy operation, it is usually possible to manage depression with a mixture of antidepressant drugs and psychotherapy. The sooner you seek help, the sooner you will be able to get back to reading.

Ways to Overcome Writers Block

Because freelance writers focus on their path to earning a living with writing, they are often in search of a list of the top ways to overcome the block of authors.

Top Ways to Overcome Writer's Block

This happens to all authors Getting stuck on a project. Luckily, you can use a lot of tricks to help you break out of the slump.

Read a Good Book

Many writers have a mixed understanding of whether or not learning is one of the easiest ways to overcome the author's disappointment. While it's true that reading in the same style as what you're focusing on can often make you feel like you don't have something unique to contribute to the discussion, reading something that's a little outside the reach of your usual content will offer you a fresh perspective that's crucial to generating new ideas. If you write romances, write some murder mysteries or a good western. Before writing science fiction, consider reading a few comic books and graphic novels. Try to read a famous autobiography if you're a newspaper journalist.

On a similar note, many people find that reading books on fiction, imagination, and authors ' biographies they admire works well as a technique to conquer the author's barrier. Many of these books also include prompts to write to allow you to express your thoughts on paper. Titles you may want to read include:

- The Complete Artist's Way: Julia Cameron's Creativity as a Spiritual Practice
- Natalie Goldberg's Writing Down the Bones
- Stephen King's Fiction
- The Five Minute Writer: Learning and Inspiration for Creative Writing by Margaret Geraghty in Five Minutes a Day

Take a shower

If you've completed an informal survey of 100 authors, you're going to have a good chance to do that. Taking a shower is a great way to get hit with a shot of energy, whether it's the warm water, your favorite body wash smell, or the simple fact that it's a bit distracted from what trouble you. You will want to keep a diary or tape recorder ready, though, so you can catch thoughts in the bathroom easily before they fail you.

Get Moving

Because of the nature of their work, writers often find themselves spending long hours in front of their desks. With one's job, lack of movement can often lead to frustration. Pump your blood and prepare your creative juices for exercise. You can try to overcome the author's block by running, going to the gym and listening to your favorite fitness game on the Nintendo Wii. Even a quick break for some stretching can be useful if you're too close to your deadline for a full workout

Examine Your Workspace

As a professional writer, you need a workspace that lets you concentrate as easily as possible on your assignments. An uncomfortable chair, poor lighting, or a computer crashing every 30 minutes can quickly lead to block problems for authors. It is possible to pay for better opportunities and take the time to fix these problems.

Don't ignore that little things like listening to your favorite music and lighting a candle in a calming perfume can also boost your mood if you're not there to distract someone. The more confident you are, the easier it is to overcome the author's obstacle.

Just Start Writing

Only start writing When all else fails, sometimes you just have to put yourself in front of your desk and promise you won't stop writing until you've overcome your problem. Because they only pay for finished work, professional freelance writers simply don't have the luxury to take weeks or months to clear the script backlog. In the media of starving writers and creative slackers, writing is like any other work, despite the pictures you see. Even if composing only 500 words a day is needed, establishing a regular schedule still works wonders.

For many readers, the first chapter is the most difficult. But if you keep plugging away at home, you will finally find a lot of useful ideas coming up. Remember, to edit your work, you can always go back later.

How-To, Self Help, and Advice Books

How-to, self-help, and consulting books How-to, self

-help, and consulting books are often overlooked as a possible source of income, but such assignments can be very lucrative for a freelance writer. While the Internet provides you with a wealth of information, people are always interested in buying books on topics like music, cooking, home repair, parenting, and dieting.

If you are interested in writing a nonfiction book, you can write with your formal training or previous job about a topic with which you have expertise. Alternatively, to share the writing credit of the novel, you may be able to interview book experts or collaborators with a single expert.

Writing Fiction

Writing the type of book you would like to read yourself is the best approach if you are interested in writing fiction. Of example, if you never read Westerns, it is impossible that a publisher wants to buy a compelling story.

Some of the fiction genres that can be found include:

- Action / Adventure

- Fantasy
- Erotica
- Suspense
- Murder
- Horror
- Historical fiction
- Science fiction
- Fantasy also overlaps genres, of course.

Of example, when trying to solve a mystery together, a book can include characters that fall in love.

Popular writing theories have some tips for fiction writers that you might find useful when brainstorming new ideas.

Don't Try to Copy Trends

Most independent amateur authors are making the mistake of thinking they could lead to a current trend and land a bestselling book. While there may be "warm" trends in the publishing industry, it is important to bear in mind that it takes a long time to write and publish a book. The publishing house is likely still trying to identify the next big idea when you see it on your favorite bookstore shelves. That's why it's best to stick to your own ideas instead of trying to stick to some great literary fad.

Where to Find Non-Fiction Inspiration

When writing a non-fiction book, it should come from your own interests and experience. At the very least, the book should be researched extensively on a subject about which you are passionate.

Further Your Credibility

Most people choose to write books because it allows them to be more authoritative and marketable in their field of expertise. Writing a book will boost your own professional standing if you are very good at what you are doing and have ideas that you will benefit people in your business.

Passion Project

Is there a subject in your discussions with other people that you seem to be the authority on an ongoing basis? If others find your views on a specific topic interesting and valuable-and you think this topic might be marketable as a novel-it might be a good option for a book topic.

Fill a Gap

If you've ever murmured to yourself, "Someone should really write a book about this," you might be the writer to make it happen. On the other hand, what can fill a gap which benefits us if you have access to information and tools that nobody else has and can turn it into a book.

Fiction Book Idea Sources

Most people write fiction books because they have a story concept. Where the story started to be inspired varies from writer to author.

- For some, it's a dream they've had, or they've witnessed a real life situation.
- For others, the book's concept comes from the age-old reading issue, "What if?" What if there was a mysterious box left at the door and everything changed? What if the heavens keep paradise by landing on a sacred staircase and it can be reached? What if every time a certain kid sneezed, people burst into flames?

- Many authors claim that the tales appear in their minds and that they are not sure where the story came from.

Write a Great Book

You may have read a book and thought like moving in a different direction would have been great for the story line— that could be the perfect starting point for your book. Of course, you don't want to plagiarize another author's work, but what you can do is be inspired by their work and create your own plot with unique characters and settings. For example, the wildly popular 50 Shades of Grey book series was the original fan fiction inspired by the Twilight series.

Follow the Story

While some authors are strictly following a book's outline, most writers feel that once they have a basic premise for a story line, they are allowing the story to go in whichever direction they think is right. Nevertheless, you may find that a short story grows into a much longer one that requires a novel, or you may discover that your plot has the potential to go completely differently, causing the desire to write a book. Only put it; only keep writing. The ideas for your book and the plot as a whole will be revealed in time.

Ideas Must Meet Realistic Expectations

Writing a book requires a lot of effort and creativity. Remember some of the less attractive information to set up for success before you decide what you want to write about:

- Decide if you want to publish yourself or try mainstream publication as this may impact how you write about.

- Know and remember your demographic while writing; for example, if you're writing for teens, avoid subjects that might exempt your book from the young adult category.

- The average word count for an adult novel is about 85,000, whereas the non-fiction book word count is about 50,000. While these are not complete laws, note when you read them.

- Recruit reliable readers to read your story and give you honest feedback — their opinions can influence the direction of your story.

Make confident that you can tell the whole story within the confines of the novel, if you intend to write a whole series.

Editors Shape and Finalize Your Ideas

The assistance of an accomplished editor will be invaluable, so prepare to find an editor to support you in the process of polishing the book. Writing a book is normally a solo task, but you don't have to finish it without some help.

Chapter 2

How To Pick The Perfect Book Idea

One of planned authors ' most normal inquiries is: "I realize I want to compose a book, however I have trouble choosing the exact point. How might I narrow down and pick the subject of my book? "There's no" one genuine way "to work out what the book will be about.

1. The Scribe Method

1. Goals: What do you, your reader and yourself want to accomplish in your book?

As an author, three basic inquiries can help you:

Question #1:

How would you like to serve your readers with your book? What are we attempting to get out of it? While your book can carry a few advantages to you, the book's substance isn't for you—it's for the reader. Readers are the book's audience, and they're going to help and sell the author, which just advantages you once it's really appreciated.

We start by having our essayists describe how they see the readers supporting their story. When you can perceive the value you can get from your adherents, you will perceive how to relate their help to your goals. Here are some normal ways essayists want to please their readers with their book:

1. Help Solve A Problem/Get Something They Want:

This is usually the enormous one, and can spread across a wide range of advantages, however the idea is that each reader purchases the book when they trust something they want will get them — so what's that?

2. Gain Knowledge/Wisdom/Information:

At times it originates from knowing something that the author wants, so it's always intimately attached to taking care of a problem, however it's not always the exact same thing.

3. Enlivened/Motivated/Empowered:

This is about how perusers are going to get a handle on strolling of the novel.

4. New Perspective:

This isn't as basic as the abovementioned, yet it is still very normal. Most essayists need an entirely different method for taking a gander at something for perusers.

Models

Types Faster and progressively proficient perusing from a book:

1. I need to move them most importantly, to influence them that they're not caught where they are presently — that they can develop and release their maximum capacity to know everything without exception, brisk

2. I might want to give them the instruments and methodologies (and after that the trust) to adapt all the more effectively. At last, I might want to open their eyes to another lifestyle, from nourishment, way of life configuration, to work. Essentially, I need to rouse them and urge them to satisfy their fantasy life.

From a book that shows ladies how to market like men, however in a good and humane way:

1. The ladies perusing this book should feel enabled to request intensely

2 for the deal. The ladies perusing this book will have the option to utilize the business techniques that I offer to expand their change rate without inclination pushy or deals y-

3. The ladies perusing this book are going to feel like, "In the event that she can do it, I can do it as well!"

4. The ladies who read this book will feel motivated to remain even with dread and go for their fantasies in deals

Question #2:

Envision it's a couple of years after your book has been distributed, the ladies who read this book will feel propelled to remain before dread and go for their fantasies in deals. How did the book help you do to attempt advantageous?

There are practically vast scopes of advantages that a book can get for an essayist, however the greater part of them can be categorized as one of these six shared objectives:

1. Bring issues to light/Profile:

Books can bring issues to light in an assortment of ways, for example, making media presentation simpler to accomplish and expanding your profile in your market.

2. Improve Authority/Legitimacy:

Books help establish authority by an author and gain believability in their calling.

3. Get New Clients/Opportunities:

Books can help generate new business and different opportunities in various ways across numerous platforms and scenes.

4. Speaking Engagements:

A book is almost an essential to turn into a paying and regularly reserved speaker for any sort of open speaking.

5. Leave a Legacy:

A book will create a legacy and pass on your story to others.

6. Impact Others:

The main issue some way or another addresses it, yet you can also bring it here. This is regularly the main advantage for certain readers. It is possible that they don't have the foggiest idea what they will get from their book, or they just care about it as a secondary advantage. Keep in mind that it has to affect others for each book to be powerful—it's simply that a few scholars put a lot greater emphasis on this than others do.

Clearly, each of these points of interest rely upon your particular field and career, however any of these targets can be realistic goals.

NOTE: The more exact the targets are, the better.

EXAMPLE

Details Read faster and all the more successfully from the same book:

1. We became our B2C business to over $10 M a year, primarily by misusing the free book channel and book coverage, while being less associated with the business than ever previously

2. We run the largest training summit on the planet, with in excess of 500 individuals paying to attend 3 a year. We accomplish more than $1 M a year in business and individual memberships thanks to the book and occasion 4's perceive ability and reputation. We have facilitated research, dialog and exchange on educational change what's more, are working together on a couple non-benefit pilot ventures to improve training From a similar book which shows ladies how to market like individuals, yet morally and genuine:

1. I have countless female businesspeople and my organization is well-regarded and known

2. I am a looked for after master on the promoting and strengthening of ladies. I was approached to talk at enormous, natural meetings, for example, SXSW and Traffic and Transformation Summit and I had a TEDx introduction. I will be solicited to address thousands from audience individuals in occasions and be paid $20 K for a discourse commitment.

3. Despite everything I get messages from individuals (ladies and men) who express gratitude toward me for composing this book since it truly helped them.

What Are Unrealistic Book Objectives?

Obviously, everyone covertly trusts that their novel will sell a huge number of duplicates and be a gigantic breakout—however on the off chance that you make that your objective, you set yourself up for frustration. These are not objectives that are reasonable. You allow your book to really succeed on the off chance that you set sensible objectives.

Indeed, the most significant thing you can do with this issue is to decimate your dreams and set feasible objectives. These are aggressive objectives:

- Sell a million books in the primary year
- Demand a TED talk
- Become an acclaimed creator
- Be a top of the line creator in the New York Times
- Get on Oprah/Ellen
- Fill an obscure enthusiastic void Here's the thing about these objectives: they're not actually unimaginable. Individuals have done every one of them. We needed to do them with a portion of our per users. Be that as it may, they're very rare, and most books don't fire at these objectives. The more you focus on practical objectives, the better the book can reach the market you have to focus to be fruitful.

By utilizing a book as an advertising apparatus, you can rake in tons of cash from an item, however that is no more. I'm discussing a few unique approaches to profit with a book here on the off chance that you need to get familiar with explicit approaches to utilize a book.

2. Audience: Whom must the book reach?

We exhort that you start with the littlest market you have to focus so as to make your book a triumph. The littler the better for generally per users. Your all our objective is an accumulation of centered circles; the pinpoint center is the essential audience.

At the point when I state little and restricted, I mean truly asking yourself, "Who is the littlest gathering of individuals to meet and effect my book?"You will ensure your book unquestionably hits SOMEONE by beginning little. A specialty approach will ensure the supporters get siphoned about your thoughts, execute your thoughts, and share your thoughts with your companions. It's not in the micro tribe any individual who doesn't meet those criteria.

The audience you have to reach is legitimately connected to the outcomes you need, and by understanding who has to think about your book to cause your outcomes to occur, you can figure out precisely who your audience is.

This strategy is not any more unpredictable than disclosing to yourself a key inquiry: "Who should care about my book to get the outcomes that I want?" These are tests for you and the per user.

For instance, if you will probably help oil and gas administrators settle on better decisions about where to burrow, and you need to talk at huge oil and gas gatherings and become the master in this area, then your audience is the individuals who book speakers for that specific meeting (and the officials who visit).

On the off chance that you will probably help CTO contract better designers and increment your believably in the CTO space to get clients for your CTO procuring organization to speak to little and medium-sized organizations, then SMB's main specialized officials are your essential audience.

In the event that you need to help individuals adapt to back torment and addition introduction in your neighborhood and carry patients to your chiropractic facility, so your audience is your locale's kin with the medical problems you can handle.

It's simple.

Genuine Examples

"Chiropractors who claim their very own organizations and are searching for better chances to sell their organizations." "Authorize purchasers who are searching for wine as a venture." "Female administrators, matured 30-45, who need to have youngsters however would prefer not to chance their employments.

 "Bad Examples:

"Ladies 20-70, battling, who need to feel much improved." "Any official who needs to be a superior head"

3. Idea: What are you going to say and why are you going to care for the audience?

The last question is the key request: what is the topic of your book and why is your user going to care for it?

This should be a quick line from your peruser that transforms into the point of convergence of the book that they have to consider.

Here are some real life examples:

Engraving Laughlin expected to help increase his profile and develop his master in the foundation preparing room where he had a history of urging. To do this, he expected to contact people who expected to get some answers concerning starting and running a foundation, and he formed the book How to Survive in Franchising, which explains exactly this.

Tyler Cauble required his capacity to be made and leads conveyed for his business land business. He expected to meet business people enthused about finding and offering rooms to do that. He did that in a book called Open for Business: The Insider's Commercial Real Estate Leasing Guide, which shares all of the nuances that business visionaries need to recognize business land.

In the tech and business endeavor organize, Jonathan Siegel expected to raise his introduction and profile, get talking gigs, and make course of action traffic. He expected to associate with tech business visionaries and investors to do that. He did all things considered by scrutinizing The San Francisco Fallacy: The Ten Fallacies Which Made Developers Fail, which nuances the stories of Jonathan building and selling twelve software associations.

Check the reactions to guarantee they work

When you answer the three request, attempt to check all of the three against each other. If you have nothing basic to exhorting the audience that you need to meet, then reexamine your book centers to contact an audience that you can reinforce.

Then once more, if your yearnings are tremendous to such a degree, that they empower you to contact an audience that isn't inside your control, you need to improve them down to something simpler so you can find an audience that you can meet.

Everything ties in together and is connected.

The needs of the watcher must be fulfilled. And if the book offers the per user interest, you can achieve the goals that you have to accomplish. In a fundamental formula, it incorporates everything. In case you look for after this, you will pick a subject of the book that offers a motivator to both you and the audience.

Part 2: The "Teach the Pain You Solve" Method

This is a methodology that I have seen work very well for certain columnists, particularly the sorts of creators with whom we work at Scribe (business visionaries, business visionaries, inventors, authorities, mentors, and so on.). It's a system that is misleadingly straightforward. That is the way by which it works: first, see a request you've had, one that caused you certifiable pain.

Second, describe the game plan with which you came to solve the issue.

Second, ask yourself, "Is this another person's worry, and accepting this is the situation, do they find my answer worthwhile?" If the suitable reaction is,' Yes, there are people who need that information,' then you're truly getting a better than average understanding of the novel. I told you that it was very straightforward. Allow me to give you a couple of cases of how this happens in certifiable books: Dr. Douglas Brackmann's

Using Your Pain to Help Others

Using Your Pain to Support Others is a brilliant book that teaches people with driven people, particularly people with ADHD, how to control their capacities and get what they need for the duration of regular day to day existence.

Dr. Brackmann formed this book as he grew up with an ADHD issue and was influenced that he had an insufficiency for as long as he can remember. He would not see it like that. He experienced his time on earth endeavoring to understand where ADHD starts from (it is hereditary in nature and has a formative explanation) and how to use the imperatives and focus that the disease produces to improve his life. She is by and by teaching the top stars, agents, Executives, ace competitors, inventors, and Navy SEALs with his time — and acknowledge how to perform shockingly better using the frameworks she expected to use to prepare for his ADHD.

He took in another ability to solve his own worry, made an association out of it, and then formed a book to share that contribution with others who experienced comparative troubles that he was.

Impact Tools You Made for Yourself to Help Other

Meetings Suck Cameron Herold is the keep going substance on the most ideal approach to hold a gathering. These systems evidently and quickly all parts of running a gathering, from setting the inspiration to what to do in case someone is late.

Herold transformed into a gathering star since when he was up to speed with expanding three firms to over $100 million in pay, no one in any of his associations made sense of how to hold a gathering. As needs be, a great deal of time and resources have been lost. It wasn't anybody's deficiency—there was no arranging, no assistance, no guide for people to go to.

And he adjusted acknowledged strategies, demonstrated his quick reports, and saw the capability of his business burst.

This is what Meetings Suck is—the instructional leaflet he has made to make the gatherings of his affiliations fun and convincing.

Problems you solve are valuable to others.

The best method to escape from home and convey your family to you by Adam Dailey is about how, in the wake of selling his association, Adam expected to dare to the most distant corners of the planet. The issue: he was hitched to four children.

Impossible?

Sorry. Likely not. Adam and his significant other were authorities on going with children: to know which air ships and hotels are ideal, to make sense of how to discover schools, to supervise daycare and meals in peculiar spots with six people, and to make the right point of view in your family to travel.

Can you see the pattern here?

The author had an issue that caused them genuine agony. They've tackled the issue in their lives.

They talked about their thought with others through a novel. The explanation it works so well is that it completes two things:

1. This makes the scholars be grounded as a general rule and to focus on something they really did. This implies they give the audience genuine worth since it is anything but a theory — it's a genuine answer for the genuine issue they have.

2. When thinking about the issue that other individuals have, the essayist ensures that they have a group of people prepared for the novel before they even distribute it.

Part 3: The "Cocktail Party Pitch" Method

Regardless of whether you can think of a book thought, the worry of numerous scholars is substantial:

Will anyone care about this book?

For over a time of involvement recorded as a hard copy and distributing books and teaming up for journalists, I've discovered an apparatus that quite often attempts to help writers answer this inquiry. It's extremely simple to do:

Envision your fantasy per user in your psyche, the accurate people your book was composed for. Presently, envision they're at a mixed drink party, and they're conversing with their companions about your book. What are they saying? This issue fits so well, since it is at the center of the creator's uneasiness. At the point when you can't envision somebody addressing their mates about your novel, which means it's not intriguing to them, and the book probably won't merit composing.

Yet, in the event that you can picture your fantasy writer addressing your mates in a reasonable and regular manner, at that point the book is presumably a smart thought. Mindfulness is the key to addressing this inquiry. Anyone can make up an inept tale about how somebody would suggest their novel. This is unhelpful. To do this, you need in all honesty with him about how individuals really address their mates for counsel.

There is a typical pattern of how and why individuals prescribe books to their family. Individuals just consider true to life books (or anything) for two reasons:

1. They removed a great deal of enthusiasm from the novel, and additionally.

2. Clarifying a book makes them look great.

For instance, if a book encourages them shed fifty pounds, they will regularly prescribe it to their companions, as individuals will commend them for losing such weight, in light of the fact that clarifying that they did it will improve their companions off.

On the off chance that the book is about how to explore the globe for $50 every day, they're going to discuss it since it tells the world that they're explorers (which reinforces their personality) and makes them look great to their companions (who are likely all voyagers).

Basically, they need to share books that make their companions look astute, educated, and front line.

This test is going the two headings. It likewise allows you to decide whether the book may be something people would prefer not to peruse. People don't share things that:

1. They're difficult to clarify and make them feel silly, and additionally.

2. Make them look quite terrible for their mates.

Of model, if the title of the book is difficult to articulate and confounding, people won't state it so anyone can hear at a gathering since they're going to feel imbecilic on the grounds that they don't have the foggiest idea how to articulate it.

On the off chance that the book is something their friends take a gander at — for instance, in the event that they're in Cross fit and the book is about how weightlifting is horrible for you — they unquestionably won't confess to understanding it, regardless of whether they truly loved it.

Regardless of whether the novel is great, however the creator neglects to portray obviously what it's about, they're more averse to prescribe it or talk about it. An inability to depict this unmistakably makes them feel absurd. At the point when you can't envision that your fantasy per user will really prescribe your novel to an alternate per user at a mixed drink party, at that point no — it is anything but a decent book thought. However, in the event that you can imagine that — by developing a practical conversational situation — at that point truly, that is a smart thought for a novel.

Chapter 3
How Do I Get Started As An Author

Essentially realizing how to begin is one of the main deterrents individuals needing to turn into a creator face. For some, trying essayists, getting moving is the hardest part. It tends to be difficult to tell what the principal move ought to be the point at which you have never distributed a book.

You must plan two main ways:

1. Outline

How you consider planning, you have to have a thought of where you're going before you start. At the point when you compose a novel, you're either an out liner or a pantser the individuals who read on their jeans ' table. (On the off chance that you compose a true to life book, the outline is guaranteed.) On the fiction side, the outline idea is clear. You are planning everything ahead of time. However panthers compose by disclosure process or, as Stephen King puts it, they "place intriguing characters with regards to provoking circumstances and read to discover what's happening." But most writers are it is possible that either (some are mixes, normally one over the other yet doing a portion of the two). In any case, you will deal with the planning procedure totally contrastingly relying upon which you are.

In case you're a genuine out liner (and an author), you will appreciate the Snowflake procedure of my companion and partner Randy Ingermanson. Be that as it may, in case you're a pantser, for non-out liners look at this article. It will tell you the best way to work in a framework while being allowed to compose on the fly.

2. Do the investigation.

Through solid research, these extraordinary stories are grounded. On the off chance that your work smells, it will sink your post. On the off chance that your legend adventures out of the Chicago Loop 10 miles east, it would be simpler for him to be in a land and/or water capable vehicle since he will be in Lake Michigan. (You considered sinking.) Do your schoolwork to stop these humiliating errors. Immerse yourself in your setting subtleties. Ensure that when it's 95 degrees outdoors, no on-screen characters wear ski coats.

Two online research resources for empower you to maintain a strategic distance from mix-ups:

- World Atlas
- A rundown of presumably the best chronological registries on earth

Don't stop your Day Job

Before I composed and circulated almost 90 books, I was definitely not a full-time independent essayist. A prepared author had revealed to me that, when I contemplated going execution, my self-used benefits should be around multiple times what I did at my work environment.

I felt paralyzed. Why much more?

He began to make reference to all that I'd need to pay for without any other individual. Everything my focal points, annuity, retirement. I generally must be careful to recognize my perusing and my office work, yet I could do some exploration during my organization off-hours.

There's no more. Each excursion would be on me. There's no persuading motivation to prevent your normal everyday employment from composing your book. Possibly you don't like it, so I prescribe that you leave it and contribute imperatives composing your novel twilight. What's the explanation? Two explanations behind doing so:

1. You will have unfaltering compensation — less to consider—when you attempt to develop your vocation in fiction.
2. The course of action would weight you into fewer hours to be progressively productive.

Also, no doubt, you can have and eat your cake as well — without burning through family time. For what, GH, you miss three hours a night? So extraordinary is that penance for your vision of composing? How seriously may you need to be a creator?

Become a Writer Ferocious About Self-Editing.

This section is essential to the point that it can decide whether the book is making an enormous sprinkle with per users and distributors—or slipping after the main page or two into the dismissal load of the printer.

Quit fooling around about altering yourself.

From the primary page, editors know whether your original copy can be dispersed. I understand it doesn't sound sane or sensible. You're stating, composing a few pages took me months, possibly years, and you haven't got to the incredible stuff!

In what limit may they do this for you? Why have they done so?

Next, in the initial two sentences, the extraordinary stuff should be. What's more, in the event that they see fifteen changes that they need to make on the initial two pages, they know the expense of altering a similar three to 400 pages will obliterate any compensation they could foresee before they even print the novel.

Your composition must be lean and mean, other than being an extraordinary story and an incredible perusing, to maintain a strategic distance from the feared "Thank you, however this does not fulfill a prompt need" email..

Here are my 21 tough self-editing rules:

1. Build a tough skin.
2. Quit clearing your mouth.
3. Select over the insensitive the typical word.
4. Overlook superfluous words.
5. Evade minor redundancies such as:"She shook her head in endorsement." It was conceivable to erase those last four sentences.
6. Disregard all over words—except if they're required.
7. Normally expel the title. Use it for explanation as it were.
8. Offer credit to the per user. When something has been set up, you don't need to rehash it.
9. Abstain from saying what's not going on.
10. Truth is stranger than fiction. Abstain from being a crazy person descriptor.
11. That is off-base. Abstain from supporting marginally grinned action words, nearly giggled, fairly grimaced, and so forth.
12. At the point when you mean allegorically, evade the term actually.
13. That is off-base. Expel an excessive amount of contribution from the stage.
14. Keep a solitary perspective (POV) for every scene.

15. Maintain a strategic distance from prosiest, not words and expressions alone, yet circumstances.
16. Oppose informative urge (RUE).
17. Seventeen. Tell, don't state.
18. Individuals talk; they're not wheezing, murmuring, crying, snorting, or answering.
19. Apply the ring of truth to actualities, even to dream.
20. Twenty-five. Elite names for comparable characters. Indeed, even a similar first name, in truth, stop.
21. Maintain a strategic distance from accentuation quirks, styles and extents.

Here are a couple of tips to enable you to propel your vocation as a creator.

1. Polish Your Skills.

In spite of the fact that to turn into an author you don't generally require conventional instruction, you need a few skills to be compelling.

You ought to guarantee that these characteristics are all together before you attempt to compose and publish your first book.

You can partake in a proper preparing project to construct certain skills, for example, my How to Write a Book and Become a Published Author program, or simply work exclusively.

2. Network with Other Authors.

Perhaps the best thing you can do to consider turning into an essayist and supporting yourself as you get moving is becoming more acquainted with other experts who are as of now working in the field.

Take part in a national or potentially virtual gathering of authors. Such experts can support you, however they can likewise give you direction and counsel while you plan to compose your first book.

3. Publish Shorter Works.

It's a smart thought to rehearse your specialty with some shorter works, for example, short stories or paper articles, before attempting to publish your first book. Attempt to publish these papers, if conceivable. In the event that you can urge authors to accomplice on littler undertakings with you, you can be genuinely sure that you will at long last have the cash and skill to compose a novel.

What sort of preparing is needed to be a creator?

Anybody with or without proper instruction can turn into an essayist. Regardless, this requires a specific measure of learning and skills.

Stop and think for a minute...

By composing an effective book proposition for a publisher, you can turn into an essayist, yet the vast majority don't think that its simple. While a few people might have the option to compose a book without setting off for college or participating in any proper preparing, some will require a degree before they can exceed expectations as an essayist in a calling. It is smarter to get a four-year college education on the off chance that you need to get a school instruction before turning into a creator. It very well may be invaluable to try out human sciences. Regardless, it might be increasingly advantageous to graduate in French, news-casting and interchanges.

Chapter 4
How To Become A Successful Writer

This will mean for a great many people having a decent comprehension of the English language, a solid information base on at least one explicit themes, and the capacity to direct examination effectively. It will likewise enable you to prepare for a profession as an essayist by learning your art. On the bedside table, the portable caution is ringing. Six: 30 a.m.

We should bolt the image in that spot before you escape rest. What are you going to do?

You're fearing the day ahead in case you're similar to every other person. You believe it will resemble mind-fumblingly exhausting work. At that point you will get up with it.

In case dislike every other person, a variety of things can proceed with your day. You're going to feel love running into you rather than dread. Your gut's fire is stirred. You can hardly wait to peruse. You realize that the minute when pen contacts paper (or contact console fingers), ground-breaking, throbbing composition streams.

Consistently, beginning tomorrow, this can occur. You should simply learn five profoundly fruitful authors' propensities. "There is preferred an existence of assurance over an existence of regret," is a knowledge pearl frequently credited to the late Jim Rohn. This is truly what great propensities are about when you think about it: consistency. Everything valuable — remaining fit, being a superior accomplice, improving the composition — is down to what you're doing, for quite a while.

Uncertain authors who compose with blasts of vitality that in the end fail out when they feel like it. We blame and rationalize their conditions, and they don't have anything to do with being a decent independent essayist or distributed writer.

Taught craftsmen produce excellence that is refined. What admirers see are their rewards for so much hard work: the shocking, gravity-challenging bounce over the stage, the magnificent lines over the canvas, or the story that carries you to an alternate time and spot.

The stubbed knees, mortifying, clear displays and letters of dismissal from the distributors is the thing that they don't see. I won't deceive you: it's difficult to keep these examples. In any case, on the off chance that you can stay with them, how much your composition will change will stun you..

Know who you are

To become a creator, and confidence accompanies this assertion. You will build up your assurance to follow up on that mindfulness. Gladly claim the name and watch the certainty take off.

Send yourself to an ace I'm a tutoring advocate. We're continually developing as craftsmen. As a writer, regardless I develop and adapt, so are numerous writers, especially the growing scholars. Sometime in the not so distant future, we as a whole need to be craftsmanship experts. In this way it is important for us to gain from the bosses. It will enable us to develop exponentially. In the beginning periods of their composition professions, most acclaimed scholars had tutors.

He had a mentor from Ernest Hemingway. As a youngster, he was tutored by Sherwood Anderson, who helped him make his first distributing arrangement. There was likewise a guide from Neil

Gaiman. Alan Moore turned into his tutor. Raymond Carver, Jay McInerney's guide, asked him to compose full time. Furthermore, the rundown proceeds.

Submit yourself to the master.

You need to appear and carry out the responsibility to be an ace of the workmanship. See it like this. You have a 9–5 occupation requiring you now and again to turn up 5 days per week or much more days. You appear at carry out the responsibility each and every day (in the event that it doesn't occur) isn't that so? Three days out of 5 days you don't choose to turn up. You risk losing your pay, or even your work, on the off chance that you don't appear without an authentic explanation.

Appear and take the necessary steps.

You need to peruse each day to be great at perusing. You can't simply peruse. You can't appear at read at regular intervals. Consistently, you read, well, consistently. I read my books, holding down work of 9–5. I've composed while I was driving. I'm continually composing for school while I'm driving. To my view, wanting just calm spots to create is an explanation not to peruse. A decent beginning stage is to decide what number of words and commitments you will compose a day. Thirty-500 words a day seem conceivable.

It's Jeff Goins. See where he's great. Nicolas Cole composes ten thousand words every day. As a creator, he's very effective. The key to turning into a fruitful essayist is congruity. In fact, it's not in every case simple, however I'm thriving to keep this standard each day in turn

Master more than one skill

In the event that I figured out how to sell them, my books could have sold better. I've taken in a couple of things about promoting and publicizing since I knew this. These aptitudes ought to be available to each creator.

I'm working on podcasting as well. I avoided it constantly. A companion of mine discloses to me it's anything but difficult to ace podcasting. It appears as though he may not be right since I'm beginning to proceed onward.

Unmistakably I'm not saying you should be an ace of all business. A long way from it, yet you will be in great stead in the event that you learn a couple of extra aptitudes to enhance your composition abilities.

Give more than you need..

Be kind and generous

It is essential to invest some energy remarking on or sharing the articles of other individuals, especially those of new bloggers and sprouting writers. Give them consolation and backing. You resembled them once an amateur. With yourrecommendation and material, be liberal. Don't simply appear in the event that you need them to purchase from you a lot of courses or books.

It's not overlooked the kindness and generosity that you show people.

When you need them, the beneficiaries will come up to buy the courses and books to make you even more successful. We all have thoughts as authors about how we want to be seen. While some writers simply want to use their writing for their personal lives as an outlet for disappointment and joy, others want to be popular for their work, but not inherently rich from it.

Others, though, want to be successful, popular, and make a good life out of it. All of these are great excuses for being an author. The main thing is to show up and do the job, no matter how you see yourself as an author. Success must eventually come with commitment and devotion.

Be willing to evolve

You're not a model since that one time a companion took a few photos of you on the sand. What's more, you're not a writer since you've composed an eBook, a couple of posts, or a web post. The level out the truth is that going from a to z requires a ton of diligent work and individual change as far as expert reading.

Each book you read, regardless of whether fiction or not, resembles an adventure. Each assignment to compose is a chance to discover some new information, regardless of how little or seemingly insignificant. Each brainstorming session and each migraine that you have encountered brings consistency to your general word type.

Define success in your own words

In your own words, consider great how would you portray a successful author?

It means being ready to compose intelligible sentences to get a point crosswise over to other individuals, or possibly selling an item. For other people, this requires being ready to pay the lease and live on the aptitudes of reading alone.

You can't prevail with regards to anything you don't define. There are a wide range of kinds of creators with a lot of success stories. Grapple with what it intends to you and be as exact as a criminologist novel author:

- Money–If it means paying for your work to be great, at that point choose how much. Is $30,000 every year or $100,000 successful? Selling 300 or 3,000,000 duplicates? The main impediments you put on yourself are those.

- Acknowledgment–in our lives, we as a whole need acknowledgment. On the off chance that reading is something for which you need to wind up popular, at that point look into the writing of the individuals who have earned their place in history.

- Society – When you measure success by the measure of life that influences your reading, portray that too. What number of fans do you have? What number of on the fan page do you like? What number of "perusers" do you have to hit your exhibition adaptation?

Write until your imagination bleeds

To be an effective creator, you should unwind into the conviction that a rather solid check of words is required.

You should peruse one for each sentence you compose. Open your heart to the work you think about deserving of achievement on a continuous premise. Consider in your specialty "great" creators to imitate and design. Discussing which... you must have a typewriting format. It's similarly as critical to characterize execution.

Personalized replication

Whatever your specialty or composing style, pick a master from inside that class and attempt to recreate one page of your best work. In case you're composing, go search and re-utilize probably the greatest post of all time. Go purchase a large print magazine for sale and utilize the papers in your very own style and in your very own words.

Any performance trainer worth his salt will ask you to practice and then duplicate what the masters are doing. Just make sure you design it so its original substance when you do it.

Have a second or third pair of eyes.

In their life, any fruitful author out there has a proofreader or editor. It's important for authors to read. Proof with proofreaders. Alter editors. That's what it resembles. In regard to proofreading the work of other men, they may be great, however not our own. Essayists can just take a riddle up until this point and then give it to another pair of eyes that can see it from an external viewpoint.

Establishing an online presence.

Nowadays, being a fruitful author somehow requires an online presence. Whatever sort of author you are, set up a site and distribute content for the utilization of the online realm. In the event that it is important to make cash as an author, at that point make certain to set up a profile for a freelance essayist. There are incalculable online individuals ready to pay you for doing the research and composing. In fact, it is staggeringly savvy to create reader bunches in the online world.

Exercise your body

I don't need to remind you why exercise is significant. Start the start in the first part of the day and fire up your motor. On the off chance that your body works great, your brain works more, so in the event that you need to improve your perusing, get some exercise.

I don't anticipate that you should run a long distance race. Remain before a column and contact your knees. Do ups push. You're doing squats. Do your Tai Chi. Accomplish something. Accomplish something. Do it at night for the initial five minutes and do it consistently.

Exercise your brain.

On the off chance that practicing is heating up physically, free composing is heating up rationally. Arriving at the running surface is hard (or for this situation arriving at the paper perusing), so this is an incredible procedure that can break difficult squares of composing.

There are a couple of various procedures for nothing composing. You can compose what's striking a chord, or work what's leaving your mouth. You can do pages in the first part of the day and obey prompts to peruse. What sort of exercise you lean toward doesn't make a difference. The fact is to compose something before you compose anything implied for the eyes of the per users.

Ask your subconscious.

Each writer travels through the squares of the colossal essayist who just won't move. You may have hit a significant point in your story. You can compose a report of a client's deals and you don't have the foggiest idea how to keep the contention strong. Make a propensity for communicating with your subconscious — it may very well be what you have to unblock your perusing.

Schedule nothing

Keeping your schedule jam-packed is tempting. A busy author is a successful author, right? Wrong. Yeah, you're a poet, but you're a maker of ideas first and foremost. If your mind is blank, ideas come to you. That's why planning time to live is critical.

Even though it's only half an hour a day, turn it all off and go out. This is one of the best practices you can cultivate in reading.

Making new connections Though writing can be incredibly satisfying, let's face it: to get some exposure, we're all in it. Therefore, to expand your network, it is important to meet as many new people as possible. It doesn't have to be in person. It's also important to reach out online. You can send an email to a fellow writer whom you respect. You can submit a pitch to one of your favorite sites for guest blogging. You may reply to a comment on a blog. Link with others on a daily basis and you will find success.

Writers can love to write so much that they neglect real success as an author involves a lot of people and things on the page outside our writing.

Chapter 5

Becoming A Successful Author

There are various approaches to characterize achievement. Give achievement a chance to be whatever "genuine" form of this passage, with one proviso for the reasons for this part: you need to have the option to compose books and win enough to bring home the bacon. In the event that you simply need a book distributed for seeing it in a shop for a couple of months (except if it succeeds it won't remain in the store always), quit your normal everyday employment and take a stab at composing the novel yourself. (Concerning genuine, I don't have a lot of foundation with composing on that line, so I can't remark on it.) So what does the success of your own novel feel like to you as an author?

Is this a huge sale of books? Acknowledgement of your expertise? Is the press featured? What about the accolades that you received from the audience? Get a call from a publisher in New York that you want your book? Being on the bestseller list of the New York Times? What's it?

You want your own book to be published?

Perhaps you'd like to write the great American book. You may want to print a collection of the old country's grandma's recipes. Perhaps you want to write a specialist monograph to improve your professional status, or maybe you have dreams of becoming a wealthy and successful author, giving up the daily grind and leading a glamorous life in a beachfront house?

For the motives, it's a lot of people's illusion and fantasy. And that's a good news here.

It is extremely easy these days. There is a rising number of independent writers selling well. The best category, he claims, is a romance style, so we ruin it, better known as "Mommy Porn." Happily, self-publishing is not just for those who want to read about girls who want to be tied up or whipped by billionaires. In a nutshell, it's incredibly easy. I'm not a techie (I compose with a fountain pen), but even I find it very straightforward to layout and upload my book, model the cover.

I don't mean a complete dismissal of traditional publishers. There are some good ones out there, I'm sure. There are great editors who collaborate with and help them build careers with new authors. There are publishers who deserve to be there. But the better the publisher, the more difficult it will be to get them to sign it. A new author had to knock on a lot of doors back in the day just to locate an agent willing to look at them-and then the agent had to knock on a lot of doors hoping to find a publisher willing to look at the book. A large portion of the original copies from obscure authors was doled out new to what the distributors called "the slush store." Of model, of "Harry Potter and the Philosopher's Stone," at most significant distributing houses, that was the truth. In authors, they all have a comprehension of what essayist accomplishment will resemble and feel like. There are rules to be viable as an essayist to get where you need to be in your vision:

1. Hang out with other authors.

Clear clamors... so where are they? Next, don't perform loner move by the essayist/writer. Most essayists are close-lipped regarding what their identity is and their books are being advertised. Inundate yourself in discussions where authors really sell books—it doesn't make a difference whether it's through the traditional non mainstream/

independently publishing street distributing route. You need to be the place the move is making place, speaking with others with basic expectations and fears — yet proceeding onward.

I was going on a voyage when my first book was three months from the time it was discharged in June. With her first book, one of the other speakers made the New York Times list. Encouraging me, I got a tune in to my new creator in three hours and you will hear an early admonishing. Goodness my, I got a mid-one—it was an early "kind," not a genuine reprimanding. Can, that sort of thing.

My desires were that when the Press reveals the book, all I needed to do was kick back and pause. No, I was told, "The minute you get off this ship, you have a lot of work to do." And I carried out a responsibility. My takeaway was significant, and with all my book methodologies it was the managing power: on the off chance that it is to be, it is up to you.

- If it will be in the media, it's up to you.
- If it's to get the presence of a book shop, it's up to you.
- If it's to get individuals to purchase marks from the book shop, it's up to you.
- If it's dependent upon you to get vows to talk, it's up to you.
- If it's dependent upon you to put myself as the "master."
- Jeeze, I composed a decent book... wasn't that adequate? No, that wasn't it. I needed to do some exploration.

2. Don't diddle and dabble..

On the off chance that distributing and being fruitful is your strategy, what's in it?

- Have you discovered your writer, book spread, inside architects and distributors?

- Which configuration would you say you are going to use for distributing, eBook, or a book recording?

- Do you realize how to distribute your book and where?

- How are you following online journals and top influencers in your class and subject?

- Have you been perusing smash hit covers and books in your class? Who makes them shine... what's more, what would you be able to emulate by adding them to yours?

- You can spend your fortune in distributing and get in on a restricted timetable. You needn't bother with a front of $1,000 in addition to—however you need one that can contrast and those hits. There are a lot of specialists who can make you sparkle... all things considered; it's to further their potential benefit that you're prevalent with one that shouts "Lift me up" to everybody. To a great extent are a bunch of dashes... yet, it's a whole deal of crescendos and valleys.

3. If you're talking about novels, think about the series.

In reality, let your book be part of a series know to the reader universe. Commit to making a novel backlist — instead of producing the first 150,000 masterpieces, is there a simple break that sets off your book #2 automatically? Start it six months from now. Write-write-write meanwhile.

Most writers of fiction would inform you that the Super Fans are not produced by book #1 or #2—it is the third one that gets their attention. You're not a one-book pony; you're an author who's here to stay, one they're going to invest in... waiting for the next book.

4. Continue to write.

Your books are the media empire's resources. Blogs, articles, spinoffs, and all social media stuff are generated from them.

Publishing keeps flowing with your thoughts and imaginative juices. Don't end there.

5. Support out other readers.

I'm a huge mentoring advocate. Just show up at conferences and be present; collaborate one-on - one with a few you link with, lead through the writing labyrinth; share tips— one that works and the ones you felt were so amazing and bomb — are essential guide posts for writers at every level.

6. Speak on your book, on your expertise.

I have never looked back on practicing the industry and realizing that the dramatic changes to traditional publishing produce less and less in copyright payouts.

The number one thing selling for me over a million books, supporting my family, paying for the education of my children, and so much more was this: SPEAK. The secret sauce was to build a speech and/or workshop around your book and expertise that prompted me to connect with millions around the world.

Speaking has taken me down avenues that I never thought about. In a small town in New York, my biggest market and buyer of books and speeches found me. Hearing what I had to say, as I spoke, a team of nurses came to me— we want you. Yes, they did, and until they told me, I didn't know it.

Throughout the year, your job, your voice, can sell books... year after year.

7. Learn how you can market your book.

Authors want... no need... to conquer the mentality of "I'd rather read" which affects so many. Publishing is a small fraction of the success of your book— it is the advertising that will seed it, fertilize it, and boost its growth. Sure, you might be a great writer. Have you any idea how many great books that died quickly before a single shoot could surface? Too many men to count.

The author's dedication to exercise the GOYT Principle... Get Off Your Tush... and realize what your target is, go to it, and communicate. If you are in a group of writers, you can quickly access it. For honing skills and brainstorming, they can be good. But if you're surrounded by writers who just love to write, who don't really care if they publish their work, you're in the wrong group. Determine what's in your bubble of success, and then build it so it floats wide and high.

Many authors would literally ask what they should do with their unconscious aloud. We clearly don't want a person to speak back to them, at least not at once. It's really about bringing up the issue where it can't hide. You can also do this by talking to a magazine, taking a walk to talk about the problem, or speaking with a trusted friend.

First, go about your work every day. If your unconscious is willing to tell you how to solve your problem, they will pipe it up on their own. For a while, putting aside the issue could lead to insight or a fresh perspective.

Holding your day jam-packed is enticing. A busy author is a successful author, right? False. False. Yeah, you're a poet, but you're a maker of ideas first and foremost. If your mind is blank, ideas come to you. That's why scheduling time to exist is important.

Even though it's only half an hour a day, turn it all off and go out. This is one of the best practices you can cultivate in reading.

Making new friends Though writing can be incredibly satisfying, let's face it: to get some exposure, we're all in it. Therefore, to expand your network, it is important to encounter as many new people as possible. It doesn't have to be in person. Even, online reaching out counts. You can email a fellow writer whom you respect. You can send a pitch to one of your favorite sites for guest blogging. You may reply to a comment on a blog. Link with others on a daily basis and you will find success.

Writers can love to write so much that we neglect real success as an author involves a lot of people and things on the page outside our writing.

Chapter 6
The Ultimate Guide to Write & Publish Your Book

I'm certain when I state that many individuals long for one day becoming a writer and publishing a book, you'll concur with me. Possibly you're one of them. If thus, you might as of now have a subject in mind, or you might even have started to write a piece.

However,: The prospect appears to be distant for a great many people interested in a profession as a writer. Be that as it may, would it be advisable for it to be? Possibly you're surprised to gain proficiency with its most certainly not.

In reality, it's harder than most imagine turning into an author and appreciate the benefits that accompany the title. It's extremely everything necessary to conquer a couple of obstacles. Simply knowing how to get moving is one of the main hindrances individuals wanting to turn into a writer face. The guide should separate the means to be taken to turn into a published author.

How do I start as an author?

For many, aspiring writers, getting going is the hardest part. It can be difficult to tell what the first move ought to be the point at which you have never published a book. Here are a couple of tips to enable you to advance as a writer in your profession.

1. Polish Your Skills

While you don't generally require conventional instruction to turn into a creator, you need a few abilities to be fruitful. You ought to guarantee that these characteristics are all together before you attempt to compose and distribute your first book.

You can partake in a conventional preparing system to construct certain abilities, for example, my How to Write a Book and Become a Published Author program, or simply work exclusively.

2. Network with Other Authors.

Probably the best thing you can do to consider turning into an essayist and supporting yourself as you get moving is becoming acquainted with other experts who are as of now working in the field. Take part in a national or potentially virtual gathering of journalists. Such specialists can support you, however they can likewise furnish you with direction and guidance while you get ready to compose your first book.

3. Write Shorter books

It is a smart thought to test the specialty with some shorter works, such as short stories or newspaper articles, before getting ready to compose your first book. Attempt to publish these writings at whatever point possible. On the off chance that you can persuade authors to accomplice on smaller projects with you, you can be genuinely sure that you will at last have the cash and expertise to compose a novel.

What kind of education to be an author is required?

Someone with or without a conventional education can become an author. Nonetheless, this requires a specific measure of information and skills.

Here's the deal...

By composing a successful book proposal for a publisher you can become an author, however for most individuals it is difficult. While some individuals might be ready to compose a book without attending a university or partaking in any conventional preparing, some will require a degree before they can exceed expectations as an essayist in a profession.

It is better to get a four-year certification on the off chance that you want to get a school education before becoming an author. It tends to be compelling for any degree in liberal arts. Nonetheless, it might be progressively beneficial to have degrees in English, journalism and correspondence. In the event that you would prefer not to return to school, investigate my book composing system to enable you to become a published author..

How to become a successful writer

To turn into a writer is somewhat not quite the same as turning into an artist. While an artist is somebody who, based alone contemplation and inclinations, composes their own books, a writer is more help arranged. Writers also produce works that are based on a customer's requests. Starting a career as a writer is near starting a career as an artist. You have to make sure that you have the correct skills before you start taking occupations.

This will mean a decent understanding of the English language for most individuals, a solid skill base relating to at least one explicit topics, and the ability to lead analysis effectively. It will also assist you with preparing for a career as a writer by practicing your craft.

What is the skill of a writer?

You need certain skills to be successful as an author. A portion of a writer's capabilities include:

1. Communication skills.

A writer must have the option to communicate with a range of readers proficiently. Contingent upon sex, age, level of education and other characteristics, audiences can contrast.

2. Spelling and grammar.

Writers ought to have brilliant spelling, grammar and vocabulary skills so that with minimal altering they can create articles, web journals and other works.

3. Imagination

Although authors often produce their takes a shot at the basis of another person's headings, imagination remains an important ability.

4. The ability to focus.

Authors is not always able to deal with tasks that are of worry to them. In any event, when they are not camped up for the subject, authors should have the option to focus on their composition.

5. Research skills.

Authors may need to supplement their expertise with research sometimes. It is an important skill for any author to have the option to direct work easily on the web or in the library.

Where are you going to start?

It can be hard to realize how to take the first step if you want to become an author... If you don't already have the expertise you want, the first thing you should do is find a way to acquire those skills.

This could mean conducting seminars or in any occasion, enrolling in school. If you already have training yet feel like you have to further improve your skills, you can practice writing alone time before looking for an occupation.

You will need to search for customers once you are ready to start writing professionally. You may attempt to find private clients all alone, or search for a third-party company that links authors to customers. You can start writing seriously once you have discovered a couple of customers.

While you are still looking for specific clients who will demand work from you, you can also make cash as an author by making your own one of a kind work and selling it to purchasers.

How to Become a Published Author.

You're an author once you've written a book. Regardless, you ought to have the option to publish a book in solicitation to become a published author. Publishing a book isn't straightforward, however if you take the right advances, you can accomplish this goal. You have two main options when publishing a book: self-publication or mainstream printing. Traditional publishing is the most usually utilized strategy. A publisher is offering you a contract with traditional publishing.

The agreement grants the author the freedom to utilize different retailers to sell the book. It will also detail how many sales you can receive by publishing the work. Independently publishing is available in several formats.

Before long, regardless of the kind of independently publishing you picked, any costs related to writing the book will be required to be charged. If you publish the book exclusively without anyone else, you will be responsible for paying all the printing, advertising, shipping, and processing costs of your book.

You can also deal with a publisher with discounts, a vanity publisher, or a publisher with print on demand. Such publishers are willing to print the book in exchange for payment and/or finished work rights.

How Do I Get a Book Published?

You should first determine what kind of publication you want to do before you can get a book published. If you're going to publish your book without anyone else, you simply need to have enough assets to get started.

However, if you're going to attempt to negotiate with a publisher, you'll have to persuade the author that your book is a wise investment. That means you'll have to apply a book draft for review to the publisher. At that point the publisher will print the book or not. Every so often, prior to publishing, the publisher can require revisions. The publisher can, in different situations, approve the book as it is or totally dismiss it.

How hard is it to be a Published Author?

It's not necessarily easy to become a published author, and it may take time. In case you're going to publish the book yourself, you'll have to raise enough cash to take care of all the related costs, which can be problematic.

In case you're going to work with a publisher, then again, you'll have to create a book that the publisher wants to persuade them that it's a beneficial effort. This may also be a long and arduous method, depending on the expectations of the publisher. Be that as it may, in case you're steady and placed your best effort into it, you'll eventually find success.

How Much Do Authors Make in a Year?

The amount of cash that a writer will get varies greatly in any single year. While a couple of authors can hardly meet terminations, others earn millions and lead experience that are totally comfortable. Most authors fall in that range some place.

The median pay for authors and writers is about $61,820 consistently, which translates into a little more than $29 an hour, according to the latest report published by the Bureau of Labor Statistics.

The most minimal earning 10% of writers earned under $30,520 a year, while the most elevated earned 10% of authors earned more than $118,760 a year. Probably the best-realized authors earn much progressively significant compensations.

Published Author Salary.

It is conceivable that becoming a published author would significantly raise your pay. It's hard to say how much you'll earn, however. As a published author, the precise pay will depend upon several things, including:

1. The Number of Books You Publish.

The number of books you write would probably increase your income as a published author by selling more books that sell well.

2. The Success of Your Book.

Your book's popularity determines how many duplicates you sell and how much cash you make. The more the book is popular, the lower your pay will be.

3. The Price of Your Book

The cost of your book will affect your pay just as the estimation of the books you sell. For actuality, more extravagant books yield more income per book. In any case, it might deflect per users from making a buy if your book is valued excessively high. Finding the correct cost point will increase your remuneration for each book you compose.

4. How Much You Earn in Royalties

The amount you win in eminences If you have distributed the book totally individually, you will get any benefits legitimately.

By and by, when you print the book utilizing a traditional publisher or another type of publisher that enables you to offer any rights to the book, you will just get a level of the benefits. The measure of salary you acquire will significantly affect your compensation.

Steps to Publish a Book

These steps are as follows:

1. Make Sure Your Book is ready

Measures to Publish a Book coming up next are the fundamental strides to distributing a book. Ensure your novel is arranged Once you start distributing a book, you have to realize you're prepared to distribute the substance you have. This guarantees you have to deliberately audit and modify the book to guarantee that it fulfills the most noteworthy guidelines. You may need the book to be inspected by other individuals before you submit it.

2. Determine How You Want to Print

The next step is to determine how to print your book. If you want to publish yourself, you'll need to find the funds. If you're interested in working with a publisher, you'll need to plan the book for different companies.

3. Get the Support You Need

Whether you're trying to write yourself or partnering with an author, you'll certainly need support. Of example, you may need to find a company to print your book if you're self-publishing. When you plan to work with a publisher, consider the publishing companies that will most likely approve your book.

How much time does editing a book take?

There is considerable variation in the amount of money needed to publish a book. Of example, if a typical publisher decides to approve your book, you will not charge the production, shipping, or warehousing expenses, and the costs will be negligible. If you choose to finance yourself, though, you can pay a couple of hundred dollars editing your book in upfront costs.

Chapter 7

How to Think As a Book Writer

It's difficult to compose a novel without the correct assistance. You could wind up committing vital errors without somebody who has done it previously. In the event that you've at any point attempted to compose a novel, you realize how it's going... for 5 minutes you're gazing at a clear page, however it resembles hours. You're up, extending, and mixing another pot of espresso to counter the fatigue.

What's more, seven days prior, somebody asks when your novel will come, and you state, "Novel? Which book? What book? I haven't got the possibility of a novel yet!"

How to write a book systematically:

1. When composing a book
2. stop procrastination. Adopt a Writer's Mentality.
3. Preparing for a Book.
4. to distribute. Space for reading plan.
5. Get book composing tools.
6. Composing your seventh book. Expel 8 Mistakes in Book Writing. Launching After Writing Your Book There are many reasons why composing a book, regardless of whether you're composing a fiction novel or true to life, places most authors in procrastination mode straightforwardly..

These are some common reasons why you procrastinate while writing a book:

- You don't know how to get moving

- In a story, emptying your heart into the universe winds up terrifying.

- You're uncertain about your composition and have a writer's square before you even started

- You're startled to get poor book surveys once you actually distribute

- You're worried that regardless of whether you write your book, nobody will read it and you'll wind up with low book sales forever

- You don't know how to take your story to transform it into a real book. Note, all the writers are directly about exactly where you are. From William Shakespeare to Walt Whitman to Stephen King, any fruitful writer started by taking a gander at a blank page.

How to Write a Book

Stage 1: Think like a Writer

When you plunk down and write a solitary word, it will be advantageous on the off chance that you take some an opportunity to answer a couple of inquiries regarding your attitude and take the correct approach.

This is one of the frequently missed strides in turning into a distributed author, which is a significant reason why so many individuals fail to finish their book. Take it from me—the consummation of these means merits your time. These will make a lot more straightforward and additionally rewarding the remainder of your book-composing knowledge.

#1 – Find Your "Why" for Writing a Book

It's difficult to compose a book without the right help. Without somebody who did it beforehand, you could end up committing significant errors. Right when you've endeavored to compose a novel at any course, you understand how it's going... You gaze at a clear page for 5 minutes, yet it feels like hours. To fight the sickness, you're up, extended, and mixing another cup of coffee.

What's more, Seven days back, somebody asks you when your novel will show up and you state, "Novel? Which book? What book? I don't have the possibility of a novel yet!" Before you open your PC and start wandering off in fantasy land about which picture taker will take the head shot of your top of the line author or be included on Oprah, you need to respond to one inquiry:

What's your motivation to compose a book?

It's inadequate to get an intriguing thought for a book. Until you put pen on paper, you need to understand your objective.

I won't swindle anyone. Forming a book is fulfilling, anyway it takes diligent work. It incorporates enthusiastic work, long evenings (early mornings), longer days, and a steady self-basic procedure not under any condition like anything you've experienced already.

It will take you through this overwhelming cycle to fortify the arrangement of your book.

Indeed, you're thinking, "I comprehend why I need to compose a book, don't perspire it. To feel significant, I need to understand it!" It's a fascinating thought, and it might be a side effect to changing it into an initiation.

By the by, basic propensities are not equivalent to your motivation— your WHY. Emotions are transient, while an objective is a more grounded, major spark to keep you devouring the 12 PM oil to crush Chapter 23 as long as the surge of sentiments disperses.

These are some popular reasons for authors to write a book

- Authority: to make a notoriety.
- Cash: monetary profit, business achievement, or living learning.
- Create a framework: interface with and work together with others in the organization.
- Love adventure: recount to an inspirational story to improve things.

A mental redirection will enable you to address genuine issues.

- To give other individuals a departure: in the event that you compose fiction, you should give other individuals a protected spot to go.
- Life-changing: books change lives, and your story will change lives for other people.

There are no wrong or right purposes for writing a book.

Your WHY will be unique to you.

You've worked out the WHY and communicated your basic expectation to compose a book. At that point directly on the sign, something will as of now take steps to disturb your advancement: your motivations to distribute.

When nothing holds you up, beginning to let pardons for not composing your book become the deterrent to your prosperity is unfortunately commonplace.

Be that as it may, it very well may be settled.

Investing a little energy talking about some basic reasons a significant number of us make to quit composing is beneficial. When the spider webs are evacuated and those mental detours are broken, you will be better arranged for the composing process ahead. Preparing your psyche is one of the initial phases in creating significant work, regardless of whether it's a digital book publishing, the next extraordinary American epic, or a venture of energy.

Excuse #1–You're not sure what to say.

You may not know it, however it merits recounting to a story.

Truly, as you read, you might be charmingly astounded to find that you have more than one story and that you havea hard time narrowing down the material. The most ideal approach to begin composing your first book is to pick a subject no sweat. You can say something regarding a book for all intents and purposes, so go with what you know.

Here's the manner by which you can discover what to expound on:

- Look at a rundown of composing prompts and story thoughts and pick a thought
- Write a rundown of the considerable number of things you're most amped up for
- Write down a rundown of all you think about
- Write down a rundown of spots you need to see as conceivable in
- Compile every one of these things and rate the thoughts arranged by what you're most energetic about.

Reason #2–There's not enough time for you.

We are generally bustling today. I'm getting a charge out of it. What's more, to what extent does it take to compose a book first? Be that as it may, I got some uplifting news: it sets aside less effort to compose a book than you might suspect. Pick something paltry an hour daily—web based life, computer games, site, and TV — and start composing. Furthermore, if there's no hour for you, attempt 30 minutes. It tends to be a wellspring of tremendous composition productivity for 5 minutes 3 times each day. Consider it. You'll be stunned at how profitable an hour daily signifies something!

Reason #3–Good journalists are expending the majority of their spare time.

To be a writer, do you think you have to peruse the entire day? Consider once more.

Likewise, to give themselves sufficient opportunity to compose, most productive writers cut down on their perusing—at any rate incidentally.

Plus, to compose an extraordinary book, you don't need to be an artistic epicurean. Your style of composing and your discourse is yours.

What's more, by plunking down and forming (not hearing what others have composed), the ideal method to find your own special composition style.

Here are a few different ways to utilize perusing to enable you to compose a book while perusing less:

- Read only a couple of sections around evening time
- Read in an unexpected type in comparison to your own (this gives you a chance to quit being excessively intensely impacted by another content)
- Be wary about what you are perusing

- Have assigned perusing time that doesn't strife with composing time
- Stop perusing for some time on the off chance that you have almost no extra time Excuse. We think.

" Goodness, I simply aren't a master. I can't expound on it. "The truth of the matter is that the entire" master "definition is close to home. The novice cosmologist wouldn't appear to be Stephen Hawking's master... be that as it may, they would be the master for 99 percent of the remainder of the world.

You don't need to thoroughly understand your subject. Inasmuch as there is a distinction of data among you and the per user—and as long as you support by disclosing to them the things they don't know to fill that hole — at that point you're proficient enough to compose a book.

So don't consider "not being an expert! "If you are excited about a subject and proficient about it, you are 100% qualified to compose a book about it.

Reason #5–You should have an ideal first draft.

A draft is a work-in-progress, and simply putting it on paper is the objective. A draft will have mistaken and that is okay — that is the thing that the procedure of self-altering is for.

Additionally, experienced proficient writers who completed a book shrouded in a manager's red pen and different red changes in a book, much the same as the one presented underneath.

As Facebook COO Sheryl Sandburg stated, "Finished is superior to consummate." It should work for your first independently published book on the off chance that it accomplishes for a multi-billion-dollar organization.

Try not to misunderstand me, as I said previously, it's diligent work perusing. However, shedding these interruptions will enable you to get the composition procedure into a positive outlook.

#3 Acknowledge You Don't Need to Be Good

A great many people consider composing a book, "I'm not an extraordinary enough writer. Until I keep composing, I need to do."

OK, I'm here to disclose to you the accompanying:

1. You needn't bother with a course in exploratory writing.
2. You needn't bother with a guide or mentor in perusing (despite the fact that it makes a difference).
3. Several great books you don't need to peruse.

Only one thing you need: a framework to complete your book. In no way like an ideal book or a decent writer can be found. The most significant qualification when you get down to it is between writers who finish their books and non-writers.

Try not to be embarrassed to be great. You should simply concentrate on your book and your composition will improve after some time.

Composing is an expertise like anything we learn. With time, it takes practice to consummate. So let go of the possibility that by perusing master composing tips and rehearsing day by day, you're bad enough and work to improve. This will persuade you to change your mentality from "I can't" to "How about we do it!"

Chapter 8

Challenges Of Being A Book Author

You haven't done that. You said you're going to. You are talking about it, dreaming of it, wondering what people would say if you finally did it. But you're here, you've not yet written a book. So why haven't you done that?

What's more, WRITING A BOOK FEEL LIKE confronting a difficult way of snags? It doesn't need to, in light of the fact that composition a book isn't what you would state about the greatest difficulties. When all is said in done, the greatest difficulties recorded as a hard copy diaries are not an absence of material, nor an absence of thoughts. Or then again that is the occasion. Not a chance. Until you distribute or need to hold up one more day/week/month/year until you perceive how this thing in which you're perusing turns out isn't a requirement for more research.

The Biggest Reasons Not To Write a Book

We should to some degree go amiss. Journalists are creators who make conditions where individuals are permitted to suffocate. However, while they might be entertainers making incredible stories out of nowhere, they likewise have their own arrangement of issues. A portion of these issues are entirely special to essayists, while others are progressively nonexclusive.

How about we list a couple of difficulties.

You have as of late distinguished the reasons why you are critical to compose a book. Get the rundown of things down, or if nothing else remember it. Did that occur? OK. Alright, OK. The rundown is only 10% of the forward movement in the battle to make you a creator. The other 90% is to discover what held you off and, to the point more, to clarify why you would prefer not to compose that book. Since you're not doing that. Or then again you'd as of now have done that.

Of extraordinary conviction, I will guarantee you that I comprehend what the difficulties are and that they separate into two arrangements of things you've been told and things you've not been told at this point. The principal reason you don't compose books is the thing that you hold in your heart subtly. We simply need to substitute the inconsequential little dreadfulness with practical, feasible data that comes to you from somebody who has by and by composed and distributed four-mass market books, various individual articles, magazine pieces, and paper duplicate.

What are these greatest difficulties creators face and their answers?

1. Editing when writing: The problem

It's baffling to be enticed to come back to crafted by the earlier day and rework it until it's fine. The downside with this is a scene is never going to be immaculate in light of the fact that you can generally discuss including and evacuating new things.

The solution

Manufacture the act of beginning when, when you plunk down to work, you left off first thing. You'll have the option to disregard the past work once you're up to speed with what you're writing right now.

2. Never-ending research: The problem.

There's far superior broad research. Be that as it may, in light of the fact that you have a book to compose, there is just so a lot of time you can give to research. You're not going to utilize being buried in work is an enormous problem.

The Solution

The methodology means to submit real time to explicit research. Check for legitimate hotspots for your work so you can complete it without spending all your time on it.

3. Distracted by the internet

The problem:[BR][BR]sitting on your PC to peruse, you wind up perusing your email, then your online life accounts. You start looking at associations gradually and you're well on your approach to sitting around idly before you know it.

Solution

You have a ton to do with the fix, so first attempt to do some research before you even sign in. You may have the option to remunerate yourself with a brief period squander after a specific measure of work. Dispose of your telephone and go to a fundamental rendition while you're perusing.

4. In love with your job The problem:

You loved building a character and loading it with every one of the characteristics you esteemed. Presently you're sitting down and wondering whether it's unrealistic. Then there are each ones of those scenes that truly don't fit into the story, yet you would prefer not to release them.

The arrangement: Choose a proofreader with an increasingly adjusted point of view that will support you. Tune in to this man, notwithstanding, on the grounds that you truly need a certain partition from your job.

5. Forgetting brilliant ideas: The problem

You're out with companions and commuting to class, and how to take care of a story problem abruptly comes to you. The vision tumbles to a clear when you're finished doing whatever you're doing.

The Solution

A propensity for keeping on you a paper scrap and a pencil will explain this issue. On the off chance that it's a lot to review, simply download an application like Color Note to effectively scribble down your musings.

6. Not taking the problem seriously.

The vast majority don't think about writing. Disregard your companions, you may find irregular outsiders condescending to catch wind of your low maintenance or all day work. It very well may overpower and disheartening.

The solution:

There's no decision yet to let your back move off the impoliteness. You may find out that they're self-important, or you may overlook their occupation. They ought to be quieted down by that..

7. Lack of partner support

if your partner doesn't believe in your work, you can find it difficult to read.Most authors face their friends and families with a lack of understanding or encouragement. If you want to write or demand that you earn more money, your partner can allocate you household chores.

The solution

Only by having a heart-to heart conversation with your partner will solve this serious problem. Report the hours

of work but also be available to meet the needs of your family. You ought to be able to work as they do!

8. Overwriting: The problem

You just don't seem to be able to stop writing even if the purpose of that particular piecehas already been clarified and done. You're not just filled with thoughts, but with words that just seem to pour out.

The solution

Find an editor, preferably a ruthless editor that reduces to a more readable level the size of your work. You can be confident that your readers will not read a book filler!

9. Not enough time to write: The problem

You may not find making the time to write seriously very easy with a full-time job, a partner, and kids. All seems to eat in your reading time.

The solution

Though gaining money and giving time to your relationships is significant, you have to brace yourself to lose any crucial relaxation. Stay diligent and intend to blend in with everything you need to do. Waking up early in the morning and having done a good piece of writing is a great way to start the day.

10. Negative feedback: The problem

You wrote a book on Amazon or Goodreads in which you poured all your heart, time, energy, and then somebody comes along and writes a nasty review. You feel tempted to respond by saying why they're right with a response.

The solution

It is best not to read these reviews at all if you are sensitive to negative feedback. Responding to any analysis, whether positive or negative, is smart. Also, please don't give your own book five stars just because nobody else has done that!

11. Dealing with the problem of rejection

So you wrote the best book you could write and want to share it with the world. You are looking for publishers but are continually being refused. This can lead to depression and anger.

The solution

Luckily, the solution is more than one way to communicate your work to your readers. Consider putting your first book out there for self-publishing. If you succeed in getting a respectable readership, advertisers will be happy to give you a second chance.Hiring a good agent always helps to make publishers appreciate the book.

12. Getting influenced on the style of writing: The question

Most styles like romance aren't serious enough for people to take you as an author seriously. This can have a major impact on your writing career.

The answer

The silver lining is that for every genre an author wants to try, there are enough takers. Every one loves everything, but focus on the people who like the genre you're writing in and target your ads on him or her.

13. The money question: The problem

You don't make much or anything from your book because you haven't finished writing it yet or your first one hasn't been well received. For many authors, this is a big problem and they sometimes give up reading in disappointment.

The solution

Continue with your day job so the money continues to come in. If you want to immerse yourself entirely in reading and not work full time, spend a few hours working as a freelance writer.

14. Social media: The question

If you're publishing yourself, you just need to get out there and do a lot of social media marketing. Twitter and Facebook, though, could suck up your time, and the whole day is gone before you know it.

The approach

Especially to advertising and catching up with fans devote a few hours each day. If you really like hanging out online, use it for yourself as a treat to complete the work of the day.

15. Your book has its own life

The dilemma that you've plotted a nice plot all out and then, in the middle of writing your story, you find that your novel has gone somewhere else, somewhere you've never expected.

The solution

There are two options you have. One, go with the current and see if it's going to be good somewhere. If not, you can go back to the original diagram. The other is to consider carefully that parts fit into your original plan and scrap the rest as tough as it might seem.

16. Interruptions

The thing you sit down to work and then somebody calls up to talk or the ringing of the doorbell. Eventually, just because they happen to be safe, someone is trying to disrupt the workday.

The answer

Say to your mates you're busy and you're going to talk to them later. For the rest of your job, you could also have the doorbell turned off, meaning potential salespeople couldn't annoy you.

17. Plagiarism: The problem

Most authors are facing this serious problem, particularly now that the Internet is a melting pot of all that mankind has ever dreamed of.

The answer

Drop an email to the person concerned and ask them to remove the dissemination of their jobs. So consider taking legal action should they refuse to do so. You've been working hard on your books and there's no reason why anyone else would take credit for it.

18. Others in your life: The problem

Your family and friends are no longer able to see you, your wife is grumbling about your absence, and your kids are not even trying to annoy you. If people are always waiting for your attention, it might seem irritating.

The answer

For your loved ones you need to make time, no matter how full the schedule is. If it's just a matter of a couple of days, you can tell them that afterwards you'll spend more time with them. But if for months it's a constant problem, then you really need to change your lifestyle so you can spend more time with your family and friends.

19. Multiple projects: The problem

You're busy at the same time with multiple projects, and then you get ideas for another book and you're forced to wonder if you're going to finish a book.

The remedy

Discipline is the answer. Although starting new projects is good, don't be the author who never finishes a project. Organize the time to keep focusing on your main current project, but you can keep making plans for your future projects.

20. USP: The problem

Hundreds of thousands of various writers ' books are on the market, and many of them are very good. There's a certain serious competition out there. What precisely are you thinking in this jungle to be noticed?

The solution

Your book is more likely to be noticed if it deals with a unique concept rather than a rehabilitation of what is already on the market. A good catchy name is another way to get noticed.

21. Writer's block

You may be struck at any moment by the Writer's block issue and you may get stuck with your story. There are various ways that the block of the author can influence you. This is, as it stands, one of the greatest challenges faced by authors.

The simplest solution

Is to take a break for a couple of days and then return to fresh work. If this doesn't work, you might be able to give a different path to your job. Consider some creative writing to get you going if you're totally out of fresh ideas.

Everything you've been taught about Writing Are you familiar with any of these sounds?

1. When you write this book, it will annoy your parents.
2. When you write this book, your sister / brother is going to say it wasn't like that.
3. Reading doesn't have any real value.
4. You have a full-time job now.

5. Real artists are starving to death. Do you want that?
6. When were you a writer?
7. What's a memoir? In all seriousness? You haven't lived long enough.
8. Wait to write until you retire.
9. I don't know how to do that.

My solutions to these are in the context of a different list.

Things you're not suggesting that you're going to need to know how to write a book

1. When you write this book, it will annoy your parents.

Maybe they could. But, let's first write it down and see what you have. Remember, don't share your job with anyone who depends on you for food, sex or protection while you're doing it. It's one of a few of my mantras. If you want a writer, find someone who's interested in your success, who's a professional reader, and who knows reading.

2. When you write this book, your sister / brother is going to say it wasn't like that.

They will. And here's your answer from this day forward: "You're right. That way it didn't occur to you. That means it occurred to me.

3. Publishing doesn't have any real value.

It has a precious quality. They share our values as they tell our stories.

4. You have a full-time job now.

Fine. You're not going to starve either. You've got to earn the compose right. You're going to write three pages a day from this day forward, five days a week. That's 15 pages a week, 60 pages a month, so in 5 months you're going to have a first draft. Solved the problem.

5. Real artists are starving to death. Do you want that?

You've got a full-time job now, remember? And if not, I'm sure you'll have time. See answer just above this one for that.

6. When were you a writer?

That's tomorrow, if you're deliberately reading it.

7. A memoir? In all seriousness? You haven't lived long enough.

What's a memory? It's not a long book which starts with your grandfather and finishes with what you've had for today's breakfast. I just want you to go into one area of your experience from here to there. You've got a hundred. Seniors from high school submit memoirs as they write essays from university. Second graders write memoirs when they write on their summer vacations about what they did. Memoir is about something that you learn after you've done it.

8. Wait for writing until you retire.

Whenever a brain surgeon tells me that when he retires, he will continue writing, I always suggest that when I retire, I will take up brain surgery. He gets the joke at times.

9. You don't know how to do that.

You're going to find out. Why are you here, right?

You must be taught to write a novel There is no guilt that you don't know how to write a book. I don't know how to construct an airplane. Were you? No one who knows how to do this is born. You must be trained. In my case, it was four of New York's finest editors who guided me, guiding me gently through my four novels, leaning in and instructing, reminding me about the need for an argument; how to set up a book; the sublime elegance of writing in three acts while writing memoirs; strong structure, pacing, pace, and more.

If in these two posts you've come this far, you're making great strides in your target. Great progress is being made. You're going there. Be sure you're on your way to your goal of writing a book right now.

Chapter 9

Self-Publishing Versus Traditional Publishing

Get inquiries from potential clients who need to compose books constantly and the principal question they regularly ask is, "Do I need to distribute myself or attempt one of the conventional distributing houses?" With a perplexing answer, it's a straightforward inquiry. To begin with, in case you're a fiction author or consider true to life, the view is altogether different. I help fiction authors every once in a while, yet the vast majority of my customers are keen on true to life.

The reaction is actually quite simple for fiction scholars: independently publishing is the best approach. That is on the grounds that, under the customary model, you can hold 70 to 80% of your book deals pay contrasted with 20%. Basic decision, correct?

The math is, in truth, the straightforward part. The rest of increasingly confounded. Here is: Both books, regardless of whether anecdotal or non-anecdotal, should be exceptionally elevated to hang out in a commercial center of something like a million books distributed in the United States alone every year. While numerous scholars believe that having a traditional publisher guarantees that the organization can deal with the limited time exercises, the truth of the matter is that a run-of-the-mill publisher will just put genuine promoting assets behind the couple of books a year that they really feel they get an opportunity to turn into a smash hit. In the event that a publisher creates a hundred books every year, one of those books is required to beat the other 99 – joined.

Along these lines, you're basically individually except if you're fortunate enough to be that one book. Now, the choice is twofold—it is possible that you can be glad to sell three duplicates of your showstopper, or you can begin another private venture: selling your splendid activity.

Inability in all honesty about this arrangement of certainties to yourself—for instance, secretly trusting that your novel will be one of those one-in - a-million smash hits is the single greatest reason for misery among writers in the wake of keeping in touch with itself.

Since, to put it plainly, it isn't likely that your conventional publisher will showcase your book, you should. Truly, in case you're a genuine creator need to be, most conventional publisher won't take you on in light of the fact that you have a good thought. I need an extraordinary thought and a spot to sell loads of books, their assertion for a way. You might be a piece of a faction that supports its kindred individuals, or you are a scholastic who can arrange the book in your extraordinarily prominent courses, selling many books a year. Or on the other hand possibly you're an open speaker agreeing with spectators around the globe to purchase your book in the wake of hearing you're giving that astonishing discourse that gives them a chance to bounce to their feet to give you the standing O and after that horde the stage.

Ordinarily, fiction authors and true to life scholars should be set up to market their own books, yet fiction essayists appear to get the thought quicker than verifiable journalists do. Actually curiously, in light of the fact that all writing in the 21st century is amusing verifiable writers ordinarily seem to have more approaches to advertise their books.

To summarize our story up until this point: fiction essayists are probably going to need to distribute themselves since they should sell themselves in any case, yet wouldn't fret doing a lot all things considered. So promptly distribute yourself and your fiction and start advertising.

Then again, genuine scholars may be best off after the customary course if—and this is a significant if—their principle target is to utilize the novel as a calling card to accomplish something different.

For what reason is it? On the off chance that you are a specialist who needs to (inconspicuously) set up your ability and along these lines better sell your counseling administrations, at that point the customary course is as yet invaluable in light of the fact that the conventional house imprimatur carries greater power and regard to your book. That way, you're going to profit.

In case you're a speaker and you need the extended talking gigs that a book will give you, at that point selling through a conventional distributing organization is significantly progressively significant. Speaker workplaces and occasion coordinators are hoping to build up aptitudes in customarily distributed books. Generally, regardless they don't consider the independently published book. Special cases exist, however it isn't astute for you to begin attempting to be the exemption.

Once more, by talking, you're going to profit. In the event that you figure you ought to distribute with a customary house presently, other than parting the capital, you should know different traps. Second, the universe of conventional distributing is difficult to split. You need an operator on the grounds that lone a beginner goes to a customary publisher legitimately, and on the off chance that you go that way, you won't get the acknowledgment you need or presentation. Tragically, representatives are nearly as troublesome as publisher to become more acquainted with.

Second, where the entire independently publishing cycle can take as meager as 30 minutes (yet I don't propose it), you're normally taking a gander at year and a half or two years with a conventional publisher.

Second, you're still in the independent publisher's problem after those two years–you must sell the novel. In the event that this is by all accounts ludicrously troublesome, at that point basically attempt to compose the novel. Maybe that is the reason despite everything we regard any stripe's creators.

Why Self-Publishing

The universe of writing has changed, and it's the ideal opportunity for you to exploit. Here are seven reasons why independently publishing is the most ideal approach—and for what reason you're going to think twice before going back to a publishing organization.

#1 – You Don't Have to Wait for Permission

You don't need to trust that anybody will give you the green light for independently published books.

- You choose when to distribute a book and how to do it.
- You determine the hands of your book.
- You determine how well you're doing.

In other words, to urge your book to enter the worldwide market, you don't need to influence any guardians.

"In any case, customary publisher don't have a smart thought what they're going to sell or not? I state, if my book gets dismissed, they're likely right that no one's going to get it. "Right.

Have you at any point found out about the novel "The 4-Hour Workweek" by Tim Ferriss? It's been a smash hit for about four years in the New York Times and the Wall Street Journal. It sold about 1.5 million duplicates and was converted into 35 dialects.

Better believe it, and get this: it was routed to the initial 26 publisher to deny it.

You may likewise have known about a book about a little youngster with a lightning jolt scar on his temple who finds he's a wizard. The "Harry Potter" establishment is a copyright success, with quickest selling books in history being the last four titles in the arrangement.

In any case, 12 publisher straight dismissed it, and it was just gotten in light of the fact that a supervisor's eight-year-old little girl solicited to peruse the rest from the book. That being said, J.K was advised after the publisher chose to print. Rowling to find a day line of work in light of the fact that in youngsters' books she had minimal opportunity to profit.

Little did they realize the publishing success they had stumbled onto?

Along these lines, simply consider the various essayists out there who began slamming in their countenances after the initial ten to twenty windows, accepting the legend they had no significant thought.

You can't enable your advancement to be chosen by other men.

Independently publishing presents you with a capacity to do that. You and your fans determine the nature of your words rather than one man in a publishing organization who may not know in their eyes the future publishing sway.

#2 – You Can Publish Your Work Quickly

If you were to present the book to a conventional publisher, it would take a long time to discharge it. Of starters, you may even need to hear back about the book proposition of as long as a half year. What's more, it will take in any event another year prior to the book is really distributed except if we endorse the solicitation.

You will create the material as effectively as you need with independently publishing. Furthermore, at whatever point you need, you can distribute another book in the Amazon Kindle store. Thus, when you construct it, you can share your work!

#3–Bring home the (aloof) Bacon

Essayists who have verifiably been composed are generally paid the measure of cash in advance. When the business come in, however, we get just a little cut in the profit.

Why? Because they have to pay the publishing house, the editor, the marketers, the designers, etc.

Be that as it may, when you sell yourself, you get the greater part of the profits (put something aside for the money you actually spend on advertising, making of books and publishing). For instance, for an eBook estimated somewhere in the range of $2.99 and $9.99, on Amazon, independently published writers get 70 percent of the eminences. That is not awful any longer!

#4–You Form Invaluable Connections

Online and face to face, independent publishers around the globe have gathered to give a network that supports each other in publishing their work. As you meet other emerging influencers such as yourself, these associations become invaluable.

"Pause, where am I going to meet these people?" Since independently publishing requires your own essayist, spread craftsman, for mater and colleagues to be recognized, you wind up connecting with individuals during your whole writing procedure.

Writers who are independently published additionally meet via web-based networking media stages like Facebook, Twitter, Instagram and Reddit. The kinship enables individuals to reach a long ways past what they could have accomplished alone or with a customary publisher they would have been confined to.

#5–You deal with your objective So a lot of a book is inspired by its motivation.

- Is there an avocation for you to profit?
- Is another profession to begin?
- Is your story going to be shared?
- Will it be an open speaker?
- Or, is your can list only something to cross?

Note, it's hard to create a novel. In addition, nothing is more dreadful than seeing the difference in your determined work into something you didn't require. You will keep up the reliability and quality of your target if you release yourself. No one drives you to sell more books and degenerate your image to attract increasingly broad groups.

You are not classified or made into someone with whom you are grieved. For you, and for you, you make. It's empowering. That is chance of autonomously distributing!

#6–Control Your Creative Concept

There are terribleness records of makers whose musings and voices ended up unrecognizable in the wake of going down the standard way. You're not just selling them your unique duplicate when you're working with a customary publisher, you're selling them your idea.

The book might be something you don't feel great with. Or on the other hand, if it doesn't meet the standard publisher's perspectives, your dreams of a continuation or revision may be completely squandered. Anyway you keep up all out inventive control as an individual maker.

With your action, you are permitted to discuss. You are protected to be troublesome or weak. You're freed to act normally. You furthermore control who you create for when you freely distribute. You can pick and after that change the classes and watchwords when you sell through the Amazon Kindle application. You assess your accomplishment in publicizing.

With 45% of computerized book bargains for new essayists, the market demonstrates that they recognize and need to buy everybody's considerations—not just those progressed by standard publisher.

#7–Influence: The Future

Many people who need to form a book need to win more money, achieve more opportunity, and offer their musings on a site.

You in like manner have all out obligation everlastingly in case you post yourself and have absolute duty regarding insights.

There is no standard circulating firm to shield you from offering an extra online course that consolidates content from your novel, beginning a talking calling, re-releasing your book with a hardcover or sound copy, or in any occasion, releasing an altered book interpretation.

At the point when you autonomously distribute, you pick the heading of your arrangement, contemplation, and future in dispersing.

Why Go With Traditional Publishing?

We at Self-Publishing School are colossal supporters of being in control and guaranteeing you get all the cash you get for the work you put on.

In this way, regular disseminating will a portion of the time be the most ideal approach to meet your prerequisites.

Here's the explanation various people would go to ordinary dispersing as opposed to collecting the autonomously distributing stimuli.

#1 – You have connections in the publishing industry

The odds of landing or making in standard disseminating are pretty much nothing.

Since this market is forceful and publisher print simply explicit sorts of books, the people who have better karma with standard appropriating are the people who have industry affiliations.

Essentially, when you meet someone in a disseminating house who is an expert or publisher, working together with the individual being referred to get conveyed through that house may be helpful to you.

#2 – You want the label

As far as customary disseminating is concerned, the best ideal position is typically that you can say you are a usually conveyed maker.

Since in order to "make it" to regular disseminating, you have to encounter different frameworks and expulsions, it will in general be seen as a sign that you are an unrivaled writer than others.

Regardless, on a standard with it may show up, it doesn't continually mean it is.

#3 – Distribution

Book allotment is incomprehensibly improved than a by and large dispersed author, generally in light of the way that you don't have to deal with any of it.

Traditional dispersing houses have very wide branches, and the book can hit a ton a more noteworthy number of shops in a bigger number of countries than if you're disseminating generally.

#4 – Less responsibility on your part

If you're the sort of person who basically needs to create the book, yet wouldn't care to consider the title, book spread structure, arranging, or continuously, by then it might be conventional for you.

Keep in mind that when you get a book deal, ordinary publisher buy the rights to your book and can make you change anything in it to suit their needs.

Toward the day's end, your plot and characters can change definitely. If you're alright with that, by then you're based on traditional dispersing.

#5 – No upfront costs to you

Keep as an essential concern this doesn't infer that traditional disseminating is thus "free." Generally, the people who recognize standard book understandings cause blunt portion in varying totals. The rest of the costs will come on the publisher starting there.

Such beginning charges, regardless, are not consistently sufficiently huge to take care of your ordinary expenses for the time frame it takes to finish the book and get it out into the business focus. Likewise, that infers you should keep focusing on another action while examining so satisfying time limitations to get your book wrapped up.

#6 – A slow and steady process

In the event that you're not in a race to get your book out into the world, at that point the long and moderate strategy of standard distributing may be gainful for you.

Ultimately, Self-Publishing Will Change Your Life

You may have ached for working with a significant name distributing house an incredible larger part, as a noteworthy number makers, and nothing will fulfill you until you get that opportunity. That is nothing out of order with it.

Regardless, assume you're winning and distributing the book lottery. There is no affirmation yet that the undertakings of your authority will get your work into book shops or into the responsibility for favored theoretical magazines or papers ' editors. There is no sureness in the volume of offers as well.

Self-conveyance, regardless, gives you an elective way. It offers you a specific motivator to get your book out there. In case your message reverberates with enough people, you have an unrivaled probability of seeing advancement in your arrangements and making an impact. Additionally, you ought to stay predictable with your book's dream.

Freely distributing enables you to shape your life into one you acknowledge, with self-rule, money, system and influence.

Reasons Why Self-Publishing Kicks Butt Over Traditional Publishing

By on 21/06/2011 with Comments 36 I understand the different sides of the condition when talking as someone who has for the most part been conveyed and freely distributed. I was invigorated when I got my first book deal, yet that energy vanished with coming about book deals. I'm getting increasingly deplorable each time a power check comes in light of the way that those reviews are tragically low relative with what I'm accepting from my autonomously distributed books. The distributing house is the one that gets every one of the prizes.

In case you are thinking about your distributing decisions, there are a couple of reasons why freely distributing rules on customary distributing—and why by and by the best time to accept accountability for your work is.

1. Make More Moola

Regular distributers charge columnists about $1.25 per copyright book all things considered. So you obtain somewhat more than a buck if your book sells for $20. You don't should be a mathematician to acknowledge you should sell a colossal measure of books with a standard distributer to truly make great pay. On the other hand, your book printing and flow costs may be around $4.00 per book when you circulate yourself. Sell a book for $20 or, contingent upon the retail outlet, you get $5 to $10 or $16 if you get it in solitude. Do I have to state more?

2. Buy Your Books at a Better Price

If you need your customary distributer to buy copies of your own books, would like to pay 40% to half off the retail cost. So if your book retails for $20, you'll no doubt pay $10 per copy in spite of the way that printing your book will cost the distributer just $2 or $3. It's hard to believe, but it's true, the makers are in like manner making money. You buy your books at cost when you appropriate yourself.

3. Book Advancements take after Unicorns

Well, book movements may not be proportional to unicorns in light of the fact that there are pushes, yet they are not as exciting as they look. Distributers nowadays set aside cash and less to purchase books (with the exception of in case you're a VIP writer or on an unscripted TV show). The ordinary writer can want to get an improvement of $5,000 to $15,000 with a first-time book deal. Exactly when the book is released, you're not going to see another nickel until you get your improvement—$1.25 without a moment's delay—until the advancement is totally fulfilled.

4. Keep up Control

Once you have cooperated with a traditional distributer, they have all the imaginative authority over your work. You can change your name, change the message, or even eradicate entire parts. All through the spread and inside structure, you would have basically zero say. It may very well unreservedly take after the organization you formed when it's set.

5. Faster Time to Market

Most standard distributers take at any rate one years to grandstand a book. You can complete your book with freely distributing and be a great idea to go in just weeks.

6. Bookstore Placement Matters Less

Benefits of standard distributing used to be that you'd get book shop plan. Regardless, a couple of reports have shown that at any rate 70 percent of book arrangements happen on the web, and that number is climbing consistently with the rising of computerized books. Lamentably, there are not so much any book shops holding tight. We never again have the effect we once had on salary.

6. Sell Your Own Ebook

Traditional Publishers need access to your print book Or advanced book, or computerized book arrangements will charge you a unimportant entirety. You will in like manner be limited from selling or circulating your book in advanced book association, and you ought to reestablish the arrangements to your distributer. It looks like leaving piles of cash on a table you can see through a glass window, anyway you can't get in touch with it.

8. You're the Marketing Agent Anyway

Most new essayists incorrectly acknowledge that a conventional distributer would expect a working activity in selling books. This is every so often apparent, grievously. You may counsel with a paid support sometimes who will book you on two or three radio shows. You can get a couple of bookmarks or exceptional fliers. However, don't anticipate much past the basics. You're starting at now expected to do most of the book headway, and in the event that you will do it regardless, why not concentrate on advancing your autonomously distributed work where you're making a huge amount of money along these lines?

9. Reprint Whatever You Want

There are 140 characters you can tweet your book to the world right this minute. On your blog or on different locales and online diaries, you can print isolates from your book. You can print and share areas at live events. Okay prefer to do this under a customary understanding for distributing? You need approval to replicate your own special work—and there's a not too bad probability that they won't let you do that.

10. Save Years of Work and Headaches

Spare Years of Work and Headaches It's agonizingly tedious to verify a customary publisher. You should initially approach specialists and editors with a letter of request. At the point when they answer, they will request a book draft, which is a record of 30 + pages that can take as long to make as your own novel, or survey sections from your original copy. You need to sit tight for an answer in the wake of presenting a solicitation. Roughly 99% of entries were declined, so despite everything you're endeavoring. Regardless of whether you secure a customer, despite everything you need to discover a publisher for that office. For a considerable length of time, this cycle can go on. Rather, every one of the additions will be discharged and harvested speedily. On the off chance that your novel is progressing admirably, you can in the end offer it to a conventional publisher in spite of the fact that you may choose you don't need it.

11. Customers Don't Know Who Printed

The Book Focus on what it resembles when looking for a book. You take a gander at the title, the name of the publisher, and the duplicate of the deals on the (or on the web) coat. Do you truly realize who composed the book? Most of the customers give little consideration to the retailer. They read audits and need to realize the book offers to them; it doesn't generally make a difference to the writer inasmuch as it's a decent perusing.

12. The Self-Publishing

Stigma Has Left the Building There was a shame behind it when independently publishing initially started to overwhelm the scene. Individuals accepted that your book was not comparable to a customary public statement. This partitioning line has obscured, in any case. So long the book is made well — it has an extraordinary spread and exhaustive altering—you have each motivation to be glad that you have assumed responsibility for it and worked your way through your composition.

So start today to compose your own smash hit.

Chapter 10
BEST Self-Publishing Companies Of 2019

It's both energizing and anxious to choose to independently publish your book toward one side; you're the ace of everything. In any case, there are such a significant number of choices you have to make, the creator, that it very well may dismay.

Another such intersection is the key choice you have to make when picking which independently publishing business is directly for you. A considerable lot of them promote their administrations to independently published creators out there. Truth be told, swimming through them is troublesome, especially when some are legitimate and some are, well, not really!

Scholars need stories to be made, impressions reported, and social association. Also, a portion of these persevering creators like their titles to be found in the spotlight.

You recollect, it's prominence for 15 minutes.

Numerous creators accept that they are the F. The day's Scott Fitzgerald or the Oscar Wilde strolling with her fledglings over a game like a grizzly. A few regarded creators need the work to be finished by the incredible customary distributers. They need the huge young men to concoct splendid spread structures, imaginative advertisers, and big shot sponsors to go to the awesome mixed drink parties and multi-city book signings.

A portion of those creators get that day when they raise the seas and the sky, or when they can't stroll over the road any longer without seeming as though they're setting off to the washroom. Sure they're getting a $1000 advance book bargain, yet they're feeling the loss of the primary composition rule.

That is, the point at which you read, you're only a writer. So if your aspiration is to assemble a busload of characters and acquaint individuals with domains meriting a dream, at that point independently publishing is for you.

In any case, we should get genuine for a minute before we go into the appealing, scrumptious bits of independently publishing. In excess of 750,000 books are distributed around the world. The vast majority state it's a million progressively like that.

The individuals who record these figures state half of those productions are independently publishing gestures of recognition. Everybody knowing this, an independently published book would sell less than 300 duplicates per year by and large, if writers line through and concoct a particular per user showcasing plan.

Several independently publishing scholars sell a great many books a year since that group of spectators reacted to the book promoting endeavors of that essayist.

Best Reasons You ought to distribute yourself.

1. You are observing your time.

The exact opposite thing any creator needs is to produce what feels like an interminable progression of letters of solicitation to get a customer. The operator is going to search for a distributer and you are promptly on a clock of time. You've been taking the snare. These suits will pull you in and anticipate that you should have stuff on a calendar that you might like.

2. You are in the Seat of the Pilot.

The spread and the cost are chosen. What's more, you don't need to change things like the name you've thought of while you've been longing for the past love interest from secondary school. You have full control. On the off chance that you need, you can continue composing your book.

3. The realms are bigger!

For each book that leaves the dispersion focus, or when Amazon tells you that your eBook is sold, you'll get all the cash. It can require up to 85 percent of customary distributing firms. You may have enough left to pay the lease, however Forbes won't call and place you on the rundown of the world's most extravagant individuals.

4. Now's The Time to Self-Publish

Now in the breeze is simply the shame and the stench distributing. Congrats to the gallant writers who have composed extraordinary books and distributed themselves, and gratitude to the Internet, all essayists can distribute themselves with a mouse click.

5. You can get the book to deal, Dude!

Indeed. It may not be that appealing to sell. In any case, a six-year-old author may do it with all the promoting apparatuses accessible. Be that as it may, by taking the necessary steps and sparing a portion of that evaluation school lunch cash you're holding under your pad, you need to do as well as you possibly can.

6. This Is the Age of Self-Empowerment and Enlightenment

What do you think? 50 Shades of Gray was composed without anyone else, and if that activity would strike it rich of the creator, you would.

Independently published books currently speak to 30% to 40% of eBook deals. Digital books themselves represent almost 40% of all books sold and are set to beat print books in the United States in 2018. This looks good for writers in independently publishing, whose most loved medium is eBooks. As an ever-increasing number of individuals grasp e-perusing, we will begin to see sound development in income. Independent publishers likewise advantage when purchasers move from physical book shops to online book shops, for example, Amazon, setting independent publishers on a level playing field with customary distributers.

That is the place the image originates from this article. We'll lead you through the business' best independently publishing firms and give you thoughts to look over, so you'll develop with an excellent book fit to be perused by the world toward the finish of the passage.

Three principle sorts of distributing administration firms However consider the two primary kinds of distributing administration firms: distributers and aggregators before you experience our rundown.

1. Retailer

A distributing organization is recorded as a book shop selling books exclusively through its own retail location. Types incorporate Kindle Direct Publishing (KDP) from Amazon and CreateSpace, iBookstore from Apple, Press from Barnes and Noble, and Kobe. By and by, a portion of these organizations have propelled exceptional projects and understandings to offer books to different wholesalers, for example, the Expanded Delivery arrangement of CreateSpace.

2. Aggregator

An aggregator not just gives eBooks a stage for distributing and retailing, yet in addition conveys them to various online retailers and libraries. It gives scholars a chance to accomplish the most stretched out conceivable degree without coding their book to the prerequisites of every distributer or dealing with a few distributer accounts. Aggregators can likewise get eBooks into outlets that journalists can not get to legitimately; for instance, Scribd, a computerized library with a membership administration and in excess of 80 million clients around the world, doesn't permit eBooks from writers straightforwardly.

Aggregators pay deals expenses from 10% to 20% for their items, well beyond the retailer's very own cut.

While the expression "aggregator" alludes to eBooks retailers, "merchant" applies to organizations making print books accessible to physical stores, libraries, and scholastic foundations, for example, IngramSpark. A few aggregators even circulate and retail print books, for example, Lulu and Bookbaby. Due to the level of relationship and the essential likenesses in what they are doing, the two gatherings can be considered "wholesalers.

3. Print-on-demand distributors

" Print-on-request suppliers notwithstanding conveyance items, these full-suite independently publishing firms give print-on-request benefits. These are particularly valuable, obviously, when you need to convey a printed book!

As we stated, all through this whole procedure you are extremely your own distributer. Which guarantees you will keep up full imaginative control of your books and settle on your business choices. For the most part, you'll get the chance to keep the majority of the benefits (most book retailers and aggregators won't charge you until a duplicate of your book really sells, and afterward they'll take an eminence cut.) But what's best for your book will rely upon your own circumstance, and that is the thing that we'll get in the remainder of this post.

Before we proceed, the exact opposite thing: know that there are unlawful independently publishing firms out there!

Best Self-Publishing Companies for Starting Your Writing Business

1. The Kindle store from Kindle Direct Publishing Amazon makes it simple for journalists to discover new crowds by distributing themselves on the Kindle site. You can transfer and send your book to Amazon for survey in under 10 minutes and inside 24-48 hours you can be on the world's biggest online commercial center. You can win up to 70 percent on your book eminences on the off chance that you are allowed to distribute yourself with KDP.

Valuing: Free to transfer Royalties: 70% if eBook costs go from $2.99 to $9.99 OR 35% if costs are beneath $2.99 Print or eBook costs? Amazon is the principal retailer on which most writers feel they could disperse their works, both the ruler of online book shops. Also, it's all things considered: it's the world's biggest online eBook retailer and Amazon.com sold around 74 percent of all eBooks purchased in the U.S. in 2015.

Fuel Direct Publishing (KDP) is the independently publishing foundation of Amazon (not to be mistaken for "Amazon

Publishing"— its division that capacities as a conventional distributer). After its mix with CreateSpace, KDP has as of late become ever greater. Any author can distribute a book without anyone else utilizing KDP, in spite of the fact that you should do it without anyone's help physically.

Keep in mind that KDP from Amazon isn't equivalent to Choose from Amazon KDP. KDP Select is the restrictive assistance of Amazon — so you can sell your book on Amazon in the event that you partake in it. Amazon will give you in return for this:

- Access to Kindle Countdown Deals and free advancements. You can limit your book for a specific time of days like clockwork— and even set it free on the Kindle store. Peruse progressively about the quality of limiting in this Reedsy Live (and the keen method to do it).
- Kindle Unlimited enlistment. KU is Amazon's readership membership administration, urging clients to peruse as much as they need. It's exceptionally well-known and nowadays a decent number of Amazon purchasers are just perusing KU books.

In the event that you have contemplated these advantages and verified that KDP Select is the course for you, at that point you don't have to peruse the remainder of this article since you essentially decided not to utilize some other independently publishing administration. Then again, you can acclimate yourself with KDP Select with these assets:

2. Apple Books:

Free to import

Royalties: 70% on most books Print or eBook?

Apple built up its independently publishing arm in 2010, one more significant name that everybody should know. Apple uncovered in 2012 that it had downloaded 400 million books on Apple Books (in spite of the fact that note that the quantity of downloads fluctuates from the quantity of books bought, as The Digital Reader portrays in this post). While Amazon has since quite a while ago obscured it as the main eBook-understanding site, Apple Books still gets many countenances.

While it might be a battle to make sense of approaches to adapt a book on Apple Books, selling one is a lot more straightforward. Apple Books gives a stage to assemble their books called iBooks Author for scholars to distribute themselves. It is moderately simple to utilize and safe to get to!

3. Barnes and Noble Publishing Pricing:

Unlimited Royalties: 65% for books sold somewhere in the range of $2.99 and $9.99 And 40% on books estimated under $2.99—more information on Print and eBook here? Barnes and Noble Press (some time ago known as NOOK Press) is the independently publishing site for Barnes and Noble, as you may anticipate. Barnes and Noble Publishing struggled to some degree notoriously with Amazon for piece of the overall industry. Concerning interfaces, however, it's anything but difficult to distribute on B&N Press — and it's allowed to transfer your novel, similar to the next enormous retailers. B&N Publishing needn't bother with selectiveness to be distributed.

Note that you can liberate your book on B&N Press of charge. Also, Barnes and Noble keeps on working and create and include new highlights for independently published creators. B&N Press just propelled a promotion entryway this January, making it simple for new writers to make advertising efforts for their books on the Barnes and

Noble site. See this page for more data about B&N press independently publishing.

4. Rakuten Kobo Pricing:

Free to import Royalties: 70% on U.S. books sold over $2.99. For books sold beneath $2.99 Print or eBook, OR 45 percent? The last huge retailer you should know is Print Rakuten Kobo. It is a Canadian organization (the Japanese web based business mammoth Rakuten's backup) thusly, it has a wide nearness on the worldwide eBook advertise. All things considered, as far as piece of the overall industry in the U.S., it is just the #5 area, in spite of the fact that it is that a seemingly endless amount of time after year.

Kobo Writing Life is simply the allowed to-utilize distributing arm of Kobo — and it's very simple to utilize! The worldwide accentuation of Kobo is likewise a decent motivating force in the event that you need to showcase the eBook to non-U.S. nations. Keep in mind, dispersing to Kobo through Kobo Writing Life (instead of an aggregator) likewise gives you a few focal points, one of which is access to some restrictive special open doors on Kobo.

In the event that you get a headache simply considering transferring your book to all these diverse book retailers without anyone else's input, that is when aggregators come into the image.

Every one of these channels can be accumulated by aggregators: moving the book to every merchant and bringing together everything into one marketing chart. For instance, with a solitary transfer to Draft2Digital, your book would be accessible available to be purchased on Amazon, B&N Press, Apple Books, Kobo — and much littler retailers.

5. Draft2Digital Pricing:

10% of the retail cost of the book sold per print Distributes to: Kindle, Apple Publishing, Barnes and Noble, Google Play Books, Kobo, Playster, Tolino, OverDrive, Scribd, Bibliotheca Print and eBook? Advanced book We lean toward Draft2Digital at Reedsy if you use an aggregator. For what reason would that be? A couple of reasons, including incredible customer support, a simple to utilize interface, and smooth web creation. Likewise, the additional perquisites that D2D brings into the course of action: they do the planning for you, paying little heed to whether you're using eBooks or printing the book's copies.

- Gives Universal Book Links (UBL) to perusers. Such UBLs, as their name suggests, make books quickly discover able by asking writers to develop a reference to all of their titles, which goes straightforwardly to the most cherished book retailer of the per user.
- Triggers an "automated back material" gadget. For your various books on each rack, this perfect thing normally adds your as of late dispersed eBook to the tab "Also by this essayist."

Incorporate the manner in which that it flows to all major eBook stores, and in Draft2Digital you have essentially the entire pack..

6. Smashwords:

15% of the retail cost on Smashwords and 10% of the retail cost on various goals sold per copy — Distributes to: Apple Books, Barnes and Noble, Scribd, Kobo, Blio, Smashwords site—Print or eBook? Advanced book Smashwords, the principal aggregator, was the undisputed ruler of the city before Draft2Digial entered the picture. Smashwords, be that as it may, is still standard today.

Smashwords and Draft2Digital offer near assessing structures and distinction in a reasonable one alongside the other assessment. Where Smashwords comes up short is its customer experience and convenience (you have to structure yourself on Smashwords, which is surely not a touch of cake). Smashwords is in like manner not passing on Amazon's books. Everything thought of it as, has a to some degree greater scattering arrange outside of Amazon than Draft2Digital, so it's up to you whether you have to exhibit your book on a part of these undeniably shrouded stores. Dave Chesson, our friend on Kindlepreneur, took a through and through look at the similarities among Smashwords and Draft2Digital that you can scrutinize here.

7. PublishDrive Premium Pricing:

10% of the retail esteem per copy sold And month to month evaluating Limited spread to: Amazon, Apple Books, Google Play, Barnes and Noble, Scribd, OverDrive, Playster, Odilo, Bookmate Print and eBook? The newcomer may be eBook PublishDrive, anyway it's absolutely profited however much as could be expected from now is the perfect time. Developed in 2015, it accessories with past what 4,500 distributers and today it can attach you to more than 400 stores. It has the different aggregators ' limits: a smooth gui and standard arrangements updates to keep awake with the most recent on your salary.

That isolates Publish Drive from the rest is:

- Options for premium valuing through Publish Drive. On the off chance that you simply consent to pay $100 every month, you will have the option to keep every one of your sovereignties, which might be a solid match for built up industry scholars.
- Their decision for conveyance. PublishDrive is additionally experienced in worldwide dispersion alongside all significant

Western wholesalers, permitting free journalists access to already wild outside business sectors.

8. StreetLibx Pricing:

10% of the retail cost of copy sold Distributes to: Amazon, Google Play, Apple Books, Barnes and Noble, Kobo, Scribd, OverDrive, Indigo, Baker and Taylor? Advanced book StreetLib, another general distributor, gives you impressively more choices if you have to meet an overall gathering of observers. It has a strong closeness in Latin America and Europe, to such a degree, that it can structure its dashboard in English, Italian, Spanish, Hindi — and anything is possible from that point! Another a legitimate model for its overall quality: it even started offering its writers things in Egypt in January 2019.

StreetLib was set up in Germany, as you may expect, yet progressing moves have been taken in the U.S. besides, the U.K. This spreads books to all huge Western retailers as of April 2019. Any maker who considers selling in European spaces or elsewhere abroad should be taken a gander at.

9. They distribute to Amazon, Apple Books, and the shop of Blurb.

Clear and yield your eBook? One of the most exceptional and accepted print-on-demand organizations out there is Print Blurb. For visual works, for instance, magazines and photo books, we particularly propose it. For a comprehensive evaluation of their convenience and photographs of the estimation of their printed books

10. BookBaby

Distributor Amazon, Google Play, Vearsa, Books from Apple, Kobo, Bookshop, Barnes and Noble, Books from Powell, and Books-A-Million.

Clear and yield your eBook? By giving a simple to utilize interface and capable customer care, BookBaby is a possibility for some freely distributing writers on the grounds that.

11. XinXii

Distributor to Ebay, Hugendubel, Angus and Robertson, Thalia, Buecher, Whitcoulls, Indigo, Kobo, Livraria Cultura, Kobo, Scribd Print and eBook? Itunes, Hugendubel, Angus and Robertson, Thalia, Buecher, Whitcoulls, Indigo, Kobo? As a general rule, EBook XinXii isn't Chinese — it is located in Berlin. All things considered, it gives universal circulation channels to journalists that may not be promptly accessible somewhere else. Keep in mind that it has a solid nearness in Germany, Switzerland, and Austria, selling in these nations to various significant retailers. The client care could be discovered needing, however, and its UI is fairly inconvenient: exchange offs that the author should make to work with XinXii.

In the long run, print-on-request retailers will end up one-stop looks for all the independently publishing needs, be it book spread structure, book conveyance, or book printing. Their eBook conveyance expenses might be high (you may test their evaluating models beneath), yet on the off chance that you need to print, compose, and sell a book, they can be incredibly helpful.

12. IngramSpark

Ingram Book Company is one of America's largest book wholesalers and outstanding amongst other independently publishing firms. However, Ingram is the nation's greatest book distributer.

Ingram is a 44-year-old organization, so it's no big surprise that IngramSpark will pursue older sibling Lightning Source's strides. Lightning Source is an accomplishment business with locales everywhere throughout the world, and IngramSpark approaches these areas.

In 2013, Ingram needed to include an easy to understand distributing stage for writers who might want to distribute a book however have restricted assets. In any case, IngramSpark accompanied every one of the instruments that Lightning Source has in its shed independently publishing stage on the independently publishing scene.

The journalists who need to rapidly get their book into the commercial center yet would prefer not to manage the complexities of mass dispersion should take a gander at IngramSpark. IngramSpark has in their composition dna the product know-how and Ingram's creation, stockpiling, and conveyance devices, and that gives numerous creators a great deal of distinction.

13. Fast Pencil

With an independently publishing house you might need to build up each part of your new book or you may require proficient assistance. In the event that you pick Fast Pencil, you can build up the fundamental pieces of your book, however there are likewise editors and visual planners on this site who have a boatload of experience to support authors create appealing material.

Snappy Pencil has the ability to make your book the quality fine art you'd long for. The stage has extraordinary apparatuses to take you with open eyes and a more than excited mentality as far as possible of the distributing procedure.

14. iUniverse

That is off-base. adores giving distributing bargains that wet numerous creators' hunger. In January, there's a 20% off arrangement going on and it merits a look. The live talk include on this page dispenses with any fear from the independently publishing of new scholars.

Before the agreement turns into an association, meeting a creator mitigates the pressure of getting to be for certain creators an independently published creator. Be that as it may, different creators are evaluated, and iUniverse isn't simply the town's least expensive distributing shop. Be that as it may, the scientists remaining by the site say they have substantially more enthusiasm for cost 14 for the uptick. NotionPress If you're an Indian novice blogger, NotionPress may be your page. NotionPress gives a scope of online assets that give writers a chance to take their composition to the following level. This site enables writers to print their book, sell it, and convey it.

New creators are given master direction in advertising. What's more, this independently publishing house, with a decent system of retailers so perusers around the globe, makes it somewhat simpler for new creators to get the consideration they need and adhere to the independently publishing procedure.

15. Xlibris loves inspiring their authors.

The elegant and appealing slick interface inspires confidence. According to some writers, the testimonials, advice, and awards that form part of the Xlibris stick are a nice bonus. But if you're trying to do business with this page, make no mistake. The core values of Xlibris. And in their presentation and packages, professionalism is the front and center.

Author activities are also part of the marketing campaign, so it's hard to ignore features on this page, particularly if you want to get the biggest bang for your greenbacks on the internet. This site has many good features, and some writers are more exposed to good features.

So which site is best for self-publishing?

- Because Amazon owns 80% of the ebook market, you can publish directly through KDP instead of going through an aggregator. For the others, you can pick an aggregator / distributor, or even momentarily ignore them if you are a new writer learning the ropes. If you go solely to Amazon, even as you earn a higher royalty rate, you can use their powerful marketing tools. Keep in mind, however, that if you exclude other stores forever, the book may never reach its potential for sales. Kobo, after all, accounts for 25% of the Canadian market, and iBooks accounts for 30% of the Australian market and 10% of the overall market. At some point in time, or for some of your books, it's best to try out all the major retailers.

- If you'd like to sell printed copies and sign up for eBooks with KDP, go to Amazon's CreateSpace. Instead, you can choose IngramSpark, Lulu, and Bookbaby because they sell print-on-demand copies and deliver them to all major eBook retailers. If you choose the above, when choosing stores from the list of your distributor, note to exclude Amazon. Without an ISBN, paper copies can not be purchased, and it's easier to get one on your own rather than using the one the printing service company gives.

- Many companies may not accept books from writers outside the United States. Processes of payment of royalty and rate of payment can also differ across businesses. See the client pages for the FAQs and contact us with direct questions.

Chapter 11

Self-Publishing Authors And

Their Level Of Income

Profiting independently publishing books isn't a get-rich plan yet you're moving to be astounded how a lot of cash you can make on Amazon if there's one online wellspring of pay that I like to discuss most, it's very independently publishing on Amazon. I'm a really unassuming person ordinarily, however I need to state... I'm shaking at distributing myself!

I've expanded my month to month pay from nothing to nearly $2 K in under three years just from selling Amazon's books... what's more, inside a year I've been making a major month.

This post about how I profit independently publishing has been one of the blog's most prominent, so I needed to refresh it with all I've learned in the course of recent years. I've included reports on the most proficient method to make your books an aloof wellspring of pay and how to make it simpler for the entire procedure.

Alright, so $2 K a month isn't enormous cash, however it arrives and it's becoming quick.

Be that as it may, independently publishing is certifiably not a protected and simple approach to profit. As per The Guardian, the normal independently published creator makes about $1,000 every year. This incorporates numerous writers with different books and a gigantic fan list.

Profiting Self-Publishing Books isn't Overnight Easy From the realistic you'll see that getting up to $1,900+ in month to month deals wasn't a story medium-term. I distributed my first book in March 2015 and in every one of the initial two months I made under $100. It wasn't until the principal entire month I made more than $500 per month to have six books out.

What amount is a month made independent of anyone else distributed creators?

Remember that each book contains about 160 pages and took somewhere in the range of 100 and 200 hours to compose. This does exclude the time it takes for an independently published book to be altered and designed or advanced for dispatch.

I was fortunate enough to locate a couple of expert consultants who can compose, plan and produce book covers at a sensible cost, yet pay more than $1,000 to print each book alone. Probably the best hotshot for spread plan and coding for consultants is by means of Fiverr.com. Costs beginning at only $5 for a plan, which means you can search out a couple of consultants without spending a ton of cash.

Be that as it may, do it right and you can profit. For both their rankings, four of my books are routinely positioned among the best five, and the little promoting that I do is all accessible by means of online life. In the course of the most recent a half year, I've reliably made over $300 per month in these books it's as yet going solid.

Giving Multiple Formats to Make Money Self-Publishing Books Just as making cash blogging includes numerous salary streams, profiting independently publishing methods giving different configurations to your book. It's helpful to sell your book on Amazon Kindle and as a soft cover since you can do it from a similar arrangement, however really improving your profit consistently means making a sound form of your book.

Comprehend that various individuals have various organizations. I adore the less expensive Kindle costs, yet numerous individuals still need a conventional soft cover book. I can never become accustomed to tuning in to a book recording, yet at least one books seven days are tuned in to by my sister.

I by and large make around a fourth of my deals on Amazon Kindle at this moment, another third on Createspace for the soft cover variant, and the other third on Audible for the sound configuration.

Transferring your book to CreateSpace is exceptionally near Kindle's strategy, the two of which are claimed by Amazon. Your book will be recorded as accessible in soft cover on its Amazon page, and when a buy is made, CreateSpace will print and mail it. Your soft cover sovereign ties will be littler after Amazon takes an offer and in the wake of delivery costs, around 30 percent.

I'm utilizing the sole arrangement with Kindle Direct Publishing, which means I can't sell my books on my gatherings or anyplace else. They get a few advantages from the special arrangement, including being a piece of the Kindle Unlimited program and somewhat higher positioning on Amazon, however this year I would likely take my books off the program. Certain locales for independently publishing to cause cash to include: Lulu, Kobo, Barnes and Noble and SmashWords, however traffic on these stages is fundamentally lower than on Amazon.

Take a gander at the video! I put in a clasp all I've found out about independently publishing, including the 10 entanglements your books will fate! Watch the video on YouTube 5 Things I've figured out how to profit Self-Publishing Books A great deal of independently publishing books that make cash comes down to the hustle. You need to distribute various books and publicize the books via web-based networking media on a progressing premise. This implies composing nearly once a day and essentially placing to profit and succeed.

In any case, there are likewise a few deceives that help you profit and distribute books without anyone else, regardless of whether on Amazon or different locales.

Equalization Self-Publishing Quantity and Quality You can't go through years idealizing and composing a book. Likewise, books that are mainstream are probably going to make less than a couple of hundred dollars every month. While the cash you make on an independently published book will be automated revenue that will keep going for quite a while, it's difficult to legitimize long periods of work for only a couple of thousand salary streams a year.

That way, not the majority of the books will profit and bunches of cash. From my very own involvement and what I've gotten notification from other independently published scholars, about portion of the books you will distribute each month will profit. Another in four of your books will profit, however you won't be eager about anything, possibly $50 to $150 every month. Just around one book in four that you compose individually will be worth more than $150 per month.

This implies you have to keep concocting these original thoughts and routinely distribute new books alone. There are two significant things to make cash by having more books:

- You're bound to hit a renowned theme and distribute a book that truly takes off

- You're exploiting Amazon's cross promotions. On the off chance that somebody buys a novel, Amazon will give them messages that prescribe different books that you've distributed, obviously, you can't simply distribute awful books and anticipate that cash should be made. I know one writer who began paying remote specialists at a pace of two every month to siphon out low-quality books. The books were absolutely horrendous, yet the cost was correct... she thought.

For the primary month she had a couple of offers, however then the surveys started to come in and decimated her notoriety on Amazon. She is presently thinking of her own books under a non de plume as nobody will purchase further books distributed under her genuine name.

On the off chance that your expertise level around a subject isn't yet loose with you, give taking a course a shot Udemy. The site gives video exercises to as meager as $15 and is an incredible method to find out about a subject.

Beginning a subject blog is likewise a decent method to assemble your reliability and aptitude in a situation before you bring the jump into independently publishing. Blogging is a characteristic fit for independently publishing capital on the grounds that your blog would carry many individuals to your book pages. Look at my 10-page Blue Host WordPress facilitating manual for all that you have to begin a blog and profit and navigate the connection here to get an uncommon arrangement including a free site title and just $3.95 a month facilitating.

A decent book discharge will rate you in Amazon, yet after the dispatch you will require a superior Amazon site to continue selling books. Not exclusively will an incredible depiction help convince individuals to purchase your independently published book, yet when they peruse for Amazon and Google, it will carry more individuals to the site. At the point when you discharge your book through Amazon Kindle Direct Publishing (KDP), you can fabricate your Amazon book page.

Beginning with the name and watchwords you pick in KDP, an extraordinary book site. Ensure you're utilizing every one of the seven of your catchphrase alternatives and invest some energy inquiring about which ones are getting loads of quests.

In a subsequent article, I will go more into watchword examine. Your title and caption ought to incorporate catchphrases, yet it shouldn't seem like you're attempting to pack it all in. The name of your Amazon book must be the genuine title, however on the off chance that you like, you can add a couple of words to the caption.

For the rundown of your novel, you are permitted to review to 4,000 characters, around 600 letters. Try not to make your definition lethargic! It's not just about delineating for individuals what the book is, yet about helping Amazon and Google find the book as individuals search. While looking, individuals will discover your book on the off chance that you utilize your watchwords in the portrayal.

H-labels are utilized to make a book portrayal stick out and get search love. This basic html code discloses to Amazon that progressively significant is a line of content.

< h2 > Using a H-Tag will accentuate the content to per users and web crawlers In the part headings of your synopsis, you need to utilize H-Tags. I utilize the main line H2 tag for my definitions and afterward the other sentence headings with H3 codes. There are other html labels that you can use to feature your depiction, however the most significant are the H-labels.

Remember to request that individuals look up and request the book! Experiencing your Amazon book outline and per users can look at the line "Clients who purchased this item additionally acquired." This damages on the off chance that they see another that looks fascinating, it may remove them from your book. Ensure that by requesting the buy you hold their consideration on your novel.

Additionally, two additional segments of your book page are significant for independently publishing cash. You should utilize the Amazon Author Central site, a different Kindle Publishing entrance from Amazon to incorporate Editorial Reviews and the' From the Writer' pages.

At the point when they come in later, you may need to include appraisals however these are a basic selling point for your novel. Evaluations of unmistakable names work best, however in any event five appraisals for your book ought to be referenced.

Purchaser remarks are likewise distributed toward the finish of the page, however don't drag individuals down before they perceive how great the book is and why they should buy it.

Your part' From the Publisher' is one of the keep going possibilities on your book to pull in a per user and profit on the site. Be conversational and clarify how it will help individuals to peruse the novel.

Pick Your Book Categories Carefully You will pick two classifications in which your book will show up when you distribute a book on Amazon. This is critical in light of the fact that when somebody is simply searching for good peruses in a sort, the book should essentially conflict with these writers.

On the off chance that you don't show up in the main twenty books, individuals won't see your book and you won't profit.

It sucks however you need to play a game on Amazon to profit. Search through a few classifications and you will see a few books that don't look proper for the class yet rate extremely high. The writer has put their book in that classification, not on the grounds that the book is the most pertinent, but since the classification isn't as aggressive as others, and the book will sell more duplicates.

You should be at any rate approximately associated with your group. It doesn't do any great to be exceptionally positioned in a classification when it's totally out of what individuals anticipate. I wouldn't bring a speculation book into a movement class, however in learning, research, or exchange, it may suit anyplace.

It's about a touch of testing to discover a segment that your book could do great.

1. Go to the principle page of the Amazon, look for "Books" to change "All Departments" and snap the glass magnifier.
2. Scroll down to where the left-hand menu shows books and all classifications. Each characterization will be parenthesized with the quantity of books, for example Photography and specialty (1,540,490)
3. Choose a couple of segments to suit your book and press exclusively.
4. Every class will be broken into sub-classifications and might be broken into classes further inside each.
5. The fewer books in a sub-class will mean less challenge for your book to rank well. I more often than not take a stab at setting my books in classifications with under 2,000 different books.

Another approach to discover that it is so focused to rank a book inside a class is by checking the Amazon Best Sellers Rank of the best 10 books. Books are positioned in this hits class against every single other book contingent upon what number of day by day deals they normal.

1. Navigate the primary books positioned in the classification where you're considering setting your book.
2. Look down to "Item Details" and find where it says "Amazon Best Sellers Rank"
3. Take the normal position of a couple of top positioning books in the classification.
4. Classifications where just Amazon Best Seller books with a position of 50,000 or lower are exceptionally focused and it will be hard to keep your book positioned in the best ten. Consider choosing a class where you just should be positioned in the best 100,000 to stay in the best ten of the classification.

Try not to Launch for Free.

This one will be dubious in light of the fact that a few people have done very well propelling their book for nothing. They make the value free for the initial couple of days and plan to get many downloads. The thought is that individuals will return to leave a survey for your book which will convince other individuals to get it when it's not free.

I gave this a shot my initial two books and detested the outcomes. Not many individuals ever leave a survey for a book, perhaps one in each 200 per users. The quantity of audits you'll generally get simply does not merit burning through the entirety of your dispatch advancement endeavors just to give the book away.

Another motivation behind why I abhor the free book dispatch procedure is on the grounds that Amazon has two diverse positioning scales for nothing and paid books. Your free book dispatch may do quite well, vaulting you to a top spot in your class... however on the free positioning scale. When you change the value, you move to the paid rankings and lose all your energy.

Propelling your book for $0.99 puts you on the paid positioning scale quickly and you won't lose all your dispatch force in the positioning once you raise the cost. You won't have the same number of duplicates surge out the entryway contrasted with the free dispatch yet you'll be profiting and will profit by positioning on the Amazon paid scale.

In the event that you can utilize your book as an approach to convince individuals to purchase different items or administrations, a procedure called a business pipe, you may do very well offering it for nothing. I know writers that make their book for all time free just to utilize it as an approach to sell different items.

Request Reviews Early.

Surveys for an independently published book are tremendously significant however constantly a writer's hardest test. Amazon says it doesn't utilize surveys or number of audits to rank a book however it is certainly something per users take a gander at before purchasing a book.

Just a small amount of the individuals that read your book will leave an audit so you're not liable to get numerous except if you are selling a huge amount of books. Rather, you have to contact bloggers and your own system for audits. You'll send them a free advanced duplicate before the dispatch and request an audit when the book is distributed on Amazon.

It's critical to ask early in light of the fact that it may take somebody a month to discover an opportunity to peruse your book and be prepared with an audit. Audits don't need to be long or point by point. They can be as short as a couple of words however a couple of sentences is in every case best. I like to get in any event ten audits inside the main month of distributing a book. More is better however getting the chance to twofold digits is typically adequate to place you in an alternate class of books from those that have only a couple of audits.

Getting audits from different bloggers, companions, and family is simpler with your initial couple of books however gets increasingly troublesome on the off chance that you are distributing regularly and consistently. Try not to be excessively pushy, simply ask more than once. Having a blog makes things simpler in light of the fact that you can connect with per users with a free duplicate as well.

I will do an entire arrangement on how I pick subjects for books and profit independently publishing books. I'll cover everything from writing to elevating and how to distribute your book on a spending limit so ensure you return in for new articles. Tell me in the remarks on the off chance that you have any inquiries regarding independently publishing on Amazon and I'll make certain to cover it.